RESIGN OR BE RESIGNED

One Educator's Response to the Challenges of Teaching Today.

MARJORIE WRIGHT

Copyright © 2009 Marjorie Wright
All rights reserved.

ISBN: 1-4392-6055-9
ISBN-13: 9781439260555
Library of Congress Control Number: 2009910267

CONTENTS

CHAPTER	PAGE
1. Migration- Counting the Cost	1
2. Education Teaches Tolerance	5
3. Time for a Change: The Push Factors	21
4. Jamaica: Evaluations, Conflicts and Resolutions	31
5. Surviving a Rigorous Recruitment Process	63
6. From Interview to Departure	117
7. Arrival in the US: The Dream and the Reality	137
8. First Day of School- The Culture Shock!	153
9. Teaching or Crowd Control- What's the Teacher's Role?	163
10. Sex, Rap and Review in the Classroom	191
11. School Bullies- Students, Parents and Administrators	213
12. Observations, Evaluations and the Teacher's Response	231
13. The Resignation	283

PREFACE

We watch the mayhem in many sectors of society and to the average person the education sector is going by smoothly, gliding like a swan. Not many people would stop to question why the swan appears to be moving so effortlessly on the water. If we were to get a picture from underneath the surface, there we would see the feet working vigorously to keep the swan afloat and to propel it smoothly across even turbulent waters. In a similar way, the hard work and endurance of teachers are often overlooked. Yet, they are the ones that keep the society afloat and mobile, in spite of the many challenges it faces daily.

Thousands of teachers are recruited to teach in the United States each year from all over the world. The US is not alone in its effort to educate its young by attracting the brightest and the best teachers. It is usually a reciprocal relationship, in which the students benefit from the best and the recruits use the opportunity to improve their position. For some, this may take the form of further studies and improvement of their art of teaching; for others it may be an opportunity to improve their lot.

The school is a microcosm of the wider society. However, just because children are younger and sometimes small people, it does not mean they have small problems. If the following headlines are anything to go by, then our future is in peril, if drastic measures are not put in place to curb the crises in our schools.

"SCHOOLS CALL POLICE 7,000 TIMES IN A YEAR"
Daily Mirror 12/23/08

"Kids of 4 Run Riot in School—Staff Just Can't Cope"
Daily Mirror 12/30/08

"15,000 Teachers off Ill Each Day"

"Three Million Pupils are let down by their schools," says Ofsted
Daily Mail Nov. 20, 2008

These were some of the issues that made news in Britain in 2008. There is no doubt that many other countries are contending with these issues as well. The **Times Educational Supplement Forums** often explore issues affecting teachers in the segment, 'What Teachers are Talking About'. After reading them for less than a year, I realize that there is a lack of awareness of some of the root causes of some of the major problems in our school systems.

In documenting my own experiences as a Jamaican school teacher, who was recruited to teach in the US, I hope to bring some of these concerns to the attention of the members of society and educational professionals in particular. I hope that this account is seen less as an indictment on our education system and more as a mirror that reflects some of the problems that need to be fixed. In the same way a mirror does not only show the faults, I have taken care to highlight some of the effective practices which should be carried out more rigorously.

This will provide educational support and professional resources for teachers. I have taken a novel approach to supplying these services, as I have presented: effective teaching and assessment strategies; examples of problems teachers encounter in the classroom and the staffroom; summaries of biased and fair evaluations, along with the Observation Checklists; examples of teacher evaluations by the students; explanation of the recruitment procedure; lesson plan ideas that work; descriptions of how to teach a five-minute lesson; and interviews, as well as other important information that teachers should know. Teachers who wish to teach abroad stand to benefit greatly from my experience. Even recruiting agencies can improve their program based on the information presented here.

The title, *Resign or Be Resigned,* runs through this work as a major theme. It is evident in my declaration that facilitators of professional development workshops, who have been doing it for years without adding anything different or new should quit or improve. It is in the suggestion that administrators should encourage and engage in more rigorous self-evaluation and improvement planning. They ought to set the pace that teachers and students will not hesitate to accept their leadership. Ultimately, it should not get to the stage where an educator feels they must give up their job or settle for mediocrity or endure whatever is meted out to them. Finally, the title hints at how ingrained some of these inefficiencies are in the schools. The ineffective management of students' behavior, the domino effect of a lack of support for the classroom teacher, the insufficient improvement in standards and the overall stagnation may mean that the only way to break the mold is to leave it and approach from another angle.

This book is written in a tone that invites the readers to draw their own conclusions and to question the establishment. The following subjects are presented: bullying of teachers by children, parents and the administration; sex and morals in the classroom; attitudes to authority, culture and the effects of the 'No Child Left Behind policy'. Many appropriate anecdotes are collocated with the main issues to make the point being made more graphic and memorable.

I was careful to include some of the most interesting incidents in my teaching career. The teachers of English will want to keep the book at hand for the lesson plan ideas. Administrators should use it as a tool to evaluate their own practices. Teachers interested in teaching abroad can see the adjustments they will have to make as well as the procedure they will go through to qualify and succeed as a recruit. Parents and students, too, can benefit from the conduct of those described. They can learn how to work with visiting teachers so that all can benefit.

CHAPTER ONE

Migration - Counting the Cost

"Marjorie, why don't you move to the States?"

Althea was taking another appreciative bite of the tantalizing ackee and salt fish, fried ripe plantain and sweet crunchy bammies, cooked to palette-pleasing delight. My fork stopped on its way to my mouth. As I paused to consider her question, I glanced at the breakfast table. The presentation was pleasing to the eye and would provoke the appetite of even the most disciplined, fasting monk. It could, probably—with a few minor adjustments—compete with the display at any five-star restaurant.

Lydia reached for a slice of mango. She bit into it, closed her eyes and chewed blissfully. A trickle of yellow juice was immediately arrested by a quick dart of her tongue. She took another bite; this time careful to lick each finger cleanly and a reassuring flick of her tongue around her lips ensured there was no more escape.

"Umm! This is good." Althea was really enjoying this country breakfast.

We had met in England three years before. I was on vacation and she was completing her degree in Accounting. After she finished, she return to life in Kingston-Jamaica and this was her first visit to my home.

"So, you don't want to live in America?" she asked between biting and moaning with the pleasure of every bite she masticated, and then swallowed.

This time the question had an air about it which made it a cross between a question and a declaration. It had lost its original interrogative quality. But she still looked at me expectantly as she chewed. It was time that I responded.

"Althea, why do *you* think I should move to the States?"

"Well," she sipped some orange juice, then prepared to take another bite. "Well, for one thing, you could make more money there…"

"True, but at what cost?"

"What do you mean 'at what cost?' Teachers are better paid there and you could always do your degree. You could have a life…" She trailed off.

I decided to ignore the suggestion that I did not have a life but such an argument merited an appropriate response. To be fair to her, I had considered the possibility of migrating, but for different reasons.

"You are right; I could make more money. But here is what I meant when I asked at what cost. Just look at the breakfast we're enjoying. You see the orange juice? I didn't buy it. You see the plantain? I didn't buy it. You see the bammies? I didn't buy them either. The orange juice was squeezed this morning from oranges we picked from our trees. Mr. Dennis gave me a whole bucket of ackee. I got enough plantains from Mitch that I could give Mary some. Mama sent bammies for me and I got these mangoes when I was out preaching door to door yesterday. Who is going to give me all these things in the States? Currently, I can take a trip overseas every year. I do not pay rent and I am privileged to be in a position to entertain friends as often as they can come. My work is just four miles down the road. I have no problems getting there. When I need extra money I can teach in the Evening School. Most importantly, I can pioneer each year. What more could I ask for?"

"You're right. I didn't look at it like that." You could tell that Althea was really mulling over these points.

"I just need to finish this house and buy a car and then I will be set for life. You know, Mitch always tell me that I have everything. She says that all I need is a little husband."

The argument was forgotten in the laughter that erupted. We all agreed that there was not a great deal I could do about that matter and proceeded to debate whether having a husband was an asset or a liability. Somehow, our conversation always seemed to come around to this issue – men! I looked around the table once again and smiled, then sighed contentedly.

CHAPTER TWO

Education Teaches Tolerance

The next three years proved to be action packed. As they say, time sure flies when you're having fun. I had enrolled at the University of the West Indies for the two-year Bachelorette program to complete a first degree in Literatures in English. The period was enlightening and I rediscovered my love for and of learning. Being a student again gave me the opportunity to reflect on my art of teaching. It was pleasing to be able to put myself and my practice under the microscope. All the different groups that I interfaced with gave some positive feedback about my contributions and it helped to boost my confidence. At the same time, I was forced to make some keen observation about some practitioners. It is true that some people will do what they have to do—not from any personal conviction, but simply because they are expected to do it. There were teachers like that in the program of study.

Who would have thought that I would have so much energy at my age? Not to be self-deprecating, but compared to the average age of the students, I was an "old foot". Most of the students were just out of high school. Some were even my former students. By this time I had been teaching for eight years.

I got a rude awakening when I went to the hall of residence. One of those in charge of orientation was a former student. Payback time! When I taught him eight years before, I was on Teaching Practice at the Manchester High School and he was in Second Form.

There was no doubt that I was very pleased to see him. What is it about a familiar face when you're in a strange place that makes you feel so reassured, so relieved? He had grown into an impressive young man. I could not have been more proud, if I were his mother. He was sporting an overgrowth of facial hair and was as cocky as ever.

We had had a wonderful time during those three months of Practice Teaching, and as I looked at him it came crowding back. The text we were studying was **The Wooing of Beppo Tate**. It is a novel written by C. Everard Palmer, set in rural Jamaica. I was in my element with lesson planning in those days. No two lessons were the same. I can't tell who had looked forward to those lessons more—the students or me. The regular classroom teacher was often present too and I tried to include her in some of my plans.

My External Assessors were quite impressed. It had felt good to look over and see that silly grin on both of their faces. They were animated as they leafed through my plans for past lessons. I was richly rewarded for my effort. Not only did I get an "A" for the practice teaching, I also got the Ken Gray Award for Innovation. This is made to the student who displays innovation in teaching strategies and entrepreneurship. I also received the

Vaughn Awards. This is for the student who best typifies the teaching profession and who displays the following qualities: a good and steady attitude to teaching as a career; useful and effective teaching skills; a healthy social attitude toward others; a combination of sound moral fiber, diligence and application to duty, as well as, the honor of being judged "most likely to succeed" as a teacher.

You can therefore understand the pride I felt at the sight of Gary Brown, my former student. If you are a teacher, then you know that feeling. Every time you see an adult who is successful—especially if you were privileged to have had an interchange during the facilitation process—you know that your chance encounter was mutually beneficial. Surely you know of students who have lost interest in a subject or school because of a poor relationship with a teacher. Sometimes it was just one incident that changed their lives forever. The same is true for teachers. They sometimes lose their joy in teaching because of students' behavior.

I was to learn from Gary this time around. When I saw him, my heart was moved with joy. It had felt so good to see a familiar face. This was University—as new students, we stood out like red kidney beans in white rice. Hoping to alleviate my own discomfort in a strange place, I greeted him and reminded him of our previous meeting. Again, I was grateful to be black—no one could see the flush that raced to my face as I absorbed his response.

"I do believe the Pressette looks familiar."

Blow me down! Did I tell you that I love to learn? Lesson: Know your place. Never fail to realize how quickly the tables can turn. I was no longer Miss Wright. For that period I was a nameless Pressette. If I were a male, I would have been Pressman. This is in honor of the A.Z. Preston Hall of residence. At the induction, you are given names. I was to be named "Chutney." A nickname has never survived with me. In high school they tried "Maroon", but it got lost. Then in College, they tried "Bugle", but that didn't live long either. *Chutney*... I thought it was a nice name, even after I heard the meaning ("your lips get hot and spicy when you eat me"). I was not thinking of anything, but chutney— the mixture of fruits and spices. Then I started to notice a pattern as I heard the meanings of the other names. There was "Dawn," for "I only come early in the morning;" "Fisherman," for "I am a masturbator;" "Grease," a name given to a female. Her meaning was, "when used Rust never comes"—Rust is another name for a male student. There were many others; some more obvious than others. The pattern was clear; all these names were innuendoes and contained debased sexual images.

Now I understood why some parents try to protect their children by not sending them to university. Although I had left my mother's home at sixteen, spent a year in the city with a wayward cousin, spent three years in teachers college and eight years on my own, I was so naïve, by their standards, it was not funny. It seemed as if, suddenly, everybody was upside-down. The brain was no longer in their heads. Every thought they uttered had something illicit permeating it.

I was reminded of the Babylonians who took the bright young men from Jerusalem and tried to indoctrinate them. Changing their names was only the beginning. The "orientation" committee indeed! They took your name, gave you one of their choice, and then they drilled and abused you for the rest of the week. According to the Super Seniors, this process was to build character. From this exercise, you were to learn self-control, so you would not fight back when abused. You would learn the discipline to stay up late at nights to complete course work, and learn to party all night as well and to be up early next morning, ready for class. Perhaps those green ones who had just finished high school needed this, but not we hardened vets who had done three years in teachers college and several years of marking students work and planning lessons late at nights, after a hard day's work.

Not to be unreasonable, I decided to learn something from the experience. Since I needed the exercise, when they got us up in the mornings, I got up and did the workout and even represented the Hall—A.Z. Preston Hall in the inter-hall events. I was voted MVP in Sports for the hall, Sportswoman of the year for Cluster Los Matadores and other awards for other activities. I was not resigned to their demands. I was in control, so I cruised with the flow, but if any rapids arose, I was prepared to change direction.

I chose what I wanted to do, but I let them think that they were making me do what they wanted. When their requests conflicted with my objectives, I drew the line. I was thus able to attend all my meetings at the Kingdom Hall and make time to prepare well for them. They no doubt recognized that I gave them everything and so Dr. Gary "Fraction" Brown had no objection. I never had to fight for my time. That was one of my guiding principles: lay the foundation early and stick to it. This same principle prevails in my classroom today. If people insist on their way and are prepared to hurt you in the process, then assess the situation and see whether it is worth the fight.

The following year I got a single room even without asking. This is as good an indication as any, that I had earned or retained their respect. I liked that.

That experience contained a valuable lesson too. Sometimes it is crucial to give a little when you want to win. You have to know when to stand and fight and when to cut and run. Running does not mean you are afraid or cowardly, but that you are aware of your limitations or what is at stake and that you are aware of, and have grasped the meaning of the maxim: he who fights and runs away, lives to fight another day. Don't think for a moment that quitting is always wrong or bad.

That was the first couple weeks as we got acculturated and acclimatized. After that we got down to the real work. Everyone had become bogged down with the real reason for being there. The lecturers reminded us often that it was not a joke nor was it a misnomer, when they say, "You're here to read for your degree." We soon found out how true that was. This was especially so in my case because I was studying literature. Was I intimidated? Oh no. I have always loved to read and, since you're reading this, you already know that I also love to write.

Certainly we met students who did very little reading and still got their degrees. There are some of those in every area of society. Often they are the ones who seem to move through the system without a hitch. They also turn up in the different sectors of society to give genuine workers a hard time. It was interesting to see how creative they became in ascribing euphemisms for their dishonesty. When we were in primary school, it was *copying*. In high school it was *helping out a situation*; in college, *bridging;* and at university, *engineering*.

More than anything else, I think people who are "honesty challenged" give rise to one of my greatest pet peeves. They are everywhere and have manipulated every available media. Sadly, it has gotten to the point where people who work hard and try their best are denied their true value. One has to learn to live by higher principles. It's one of the reasons I like the Bible character Job. He said, "Until I expire I will not take away my integrity from myself." Ultimately, that is what matters. An individual has to be true to himself. Because of the arrangement of the system where a person may be disqualified although he has the qualification, you have to develop higher qualities; qualities that can't be taken from you. Live by the undeniable truth to be true to yourself. My conviction dictated that I did my best at everything, school work, volunteer activities such as reading for the blind and helping with homework at the Mona Rehab, ministering from door to door or playing games for the hall. I still marvel at the things I got done while on campus during those two years.

At the end of the program I thought I needed a well deserved and a well earned break. You would probably agree, but, as life usually has it, there were those in opposition. I wanted to travel so I set about securing my visas. When the USA embassy turned me down, there was no surprise. This was the third time. They didn't even make their reason seem logical.

When I arrived at the embassy, there was a line that snaked around the corner in the beaming sun. I was taken aback by this sight because we all had to make an appointment. I could not understand why they would arrange for so many people to arrive at the same time.

The police on guard dutifully informed us as we approached, that we were not allowed to take electronic devices and keys on the grounds. What do I do with my room key and my cell phone at this point? This is Jamaica, people are innovative. Already there were touts with a system of securing our personal effects. You paid one hundred dollars and they collected them and gave you a ticket. They placed these in a bag with your number attached until you were ready to leave. You then proceeded through the gates and moved as the long line moved slowly in the hot sun like a snake recoiling slowly through the gates, around the corner, up the incline and under the awning. Shade at last—cool shade at last! Your documents are checked and you finally get to a door.

Here you take off your shoes and belt and anything else they ask you to remove, before you are scanned. When you enter the room, you are pointed to chairs. This is where the game of musical chairs begins as you move from row to row of chairs until you go up stairs. Upstairs you do another dance of musical chairs before you join the Conga line. Here I usually spend the least amount of time. It is as easy as this, after the greeting: "Miss Wright, are you married?"

"No."

This is information I spent valuable time filling in on the visa application form.

"Do you have any children?"

"No."

This was answered on the form as well—let's give them the benefit of the doubt. But let me ask you, do you really think they read these things? Why don't they ask me why I visited Cuba; or one of those other objectionable points that could give pause? She turned to a section on the form—now she reads.

"I see that your father is a citizen in the States; why hasn't he filed for you?"

You and I know that this is not done overnight. When you start those processes, life goes on. There are things you do in the meantime.

"We have considered it, but I wanted to complete my course of study here."

"I'm sorry Miss Wright, but we are unable to grant you a visa at this time. When your situation changes, you may wish to reapply."

That was it.

With that she stamped and returned my passport, gave me a letter telling me how to reapply, wished me a good day and was ready for the next—prospect or victim? I turned and watched the faces of the others in the line. Most turned away in sorrow and fear. Fear perhaps, that they may see their fate mirrored on my face. My dashed opportunity was now a mirror of their feelings. I smiled at some friends I had found while waiting and wished them all the best. I don't mind failing so much, it is usually the people who make up rules as they go along that get to me. Let me lose fairly and I can live with it; when I lose unfairly we both have to live with it. People really only cheat themselves when they attempt to cheat you.

Do you see the task ahead of me? If I'm to get a visa to the USA, I needed to change my situation. If those questions were any clue, I needed to get married, have children or have my father file for me. When was having a mate or children a deterrent for people to remain on the right side of the law?

The British Consulate was a different and more pleasant experience. By comparison to the visit to the US Embassy, it was painless. The expression I thought of at the time was, more humane. I had sent the application through a travel agent. The Consulate called to confirm my appointment. I arrived on time and sat on benches on the compound to wait. We did our security bit then proceeded to the building for the interview. I was able to keep my keys and my phone. There were fewer people waiting than there were at the US Embassy.

When it was time for my interview, I was asked to sit. I sat across from the interviewer and I felt comfortable. She went through the preliminaries then the serious matters. I explained that I had just finished studying and wanted to take a break, but also to have a learning experience. Since I was teaching English language and English literature, it was only fair that I should visit the place where I might begin to have a more intimate knowledge and develop a deeper appreciation of my subject.

When I visited the first time, the Shakespearean Globe Theater was undergoing repairs and the London's Eye was under construction; but there were so many other places I wanted to go and things I wanted to do.

She commended me for successfully completing my course of study. We chatted a little about our separate visits to the Cayman Islands, after which she expressed the wish that I would enjoy my visit to England and be able to accomplish the activities I had outlined. She smiled brightly as she typed away on her most unusual keyboard. Her Asian eyes crinkled as she smiled and I knew she was genuine. She seemed to enjoy her job and was good at making her client feel at ease. You know, even if they had turned me down, I would not have felt badly about the experience.

You are probably wondering how it was possible for me to be going off abroad having just completed two years in university. I had become something of a shrewd business woman over the years. I had saved to pay my fees for the first year. Because I had not taught for ten years and I had taken my vacation leave after the first five years, I could only receive one year Study Leave with pay. Therefore, I applied for two years study leave and stipulated that my payment would begin in the second year. In my second year I took a loan from the bank, because I could not circumnavigate the rigmarole of the Students' Loan Bureau. In fact, the first morning I went to the SLB, I could not believe what I saw. There were people there who had stayed overnight so they could get in line and be among the first to be considered. The sight reminded me of those scenes on the television of refugee camps when people are forced to leave home and make do elsewhere.

By the time it was time to graduate, I was paying back my loan through a direct deposit system and a standing order. Since I was cutting costs, I did not attend the graduation exercise; it would mean subsidizing most of those of my relatives who would want to attend. The graduation package was just not worth it in my view. The cost was more than I could afford. It was easier that way.

I made a choice between the Award Ceremony and the Graduation Ceremony. Life is about choices all the time. I was off for three wonderful adventurous months of English summer vacation.

They say that, if you are positive, ambitious and goal-oriented, the universe will conspire to ensure that you succeed. Can I vouch for that? You bet I can. By the time I had returned to Jamaica, I had it all planned. With the house practically finished, I was in a position to buy a car. I applied for my tax returns and, when I received them, I combined them with my savings. The car wouldn't be new, but it would be better than road worthy; and it would be mine. It would be in good condition, at a price I could afford. The idea of taking out another loan held no appeal for me.

After much ado, promises made and broken, my patience threatening to desert me, I was able to secure a 1996, used, hatchback, Suzuki Swift. If I'm to be honest with you, I was not exactly enthralled at the sight of it. The dealer repainted it, changed a few damaged parts and had an air conditioner installed. I live in Santa Cruz, one of the five plains in Jamaica and famous as the hottest place on the island; therefore, I needed the AC in working order.

The dealer and I shook hands, exchanged receipts and said our goodbyes. The Swift—soon to be named "Emperor"—and I went on to have a most unforgettable two years together. I will save some of our adventure for some other account; you can't miss these stories from our first night when I backed into a pimento tree, to floating through flood waters, Emperor running away one night, losing the brake and disc pads in the middle of traffic on the busy roads in Cross Roads in Kingston to selling Emperor. Yes, selling Emperor—*sniff!*

Emperor was not to be the sole entry into my life and experience that year. From the outset I was committed to teaching for two years after graduation. The plan was to teach for two years; then take three years off to live and work abroad, acquire my masters; then return home and start my business. This would allow me to do what I have always wanted to do: spend more time in the ministry.

My life seemed to be divided in two years segments. From September 2004 to August 2005, I would become host to three little girls, aged five, eight and twelve. Most of my friends think that I have gained a degree in motherhood; others think that I am merely a certified nut. I never told those girls or their mothers this, but it was an inestimable privilege to have been able to care for them. The cord of love is now wound tightly around my heart. Those nights of waking up to check on them to make sure they were breathing, making time for homework, play, teaching them to make jelly, to wash their socks and panties, the visits to the doctors, after school pickups are just a few of the things I remember with fondness now.

After the girls left, it should have been some "me time," but you know what they say: "A good teacher is like a candle. It consumes itself to light the way for others." Before I knew it, I had four teen age boys to accommodate for a few months.

Sometimes I don't think too much. I live by some guiding principles and if I apply them to a problem and there are no conflicts, then I act. If there is a problem, usually there is a solution. Quickly, I prayerfully explore the situation and arrive at what is usually a logical and practical response. People often say I make things seem too simple. Why do some people think it can only work if it appears complicated? Simple works for me—life is not easy, but it is simple.

There was a problem. The school's dormitory had been destroyed by the recent hurricane. The boys had to study for the School's Challenge Quiz. This is the longest running game show of its kind in the Caribbean. Schools are made and broken by their reputation in this competition. Our school was relatively new at it, but they had shown improvement over the short period. They were making a name for themselves especially because it is a technical school.

Because I was overbooked in assigned classes; I had five grade nines, once-per-week for literature; one grade ten, three times for English; two grade elevens, three times for English Language, as they were preparing for the Caribbean Examination Council and GCSE examinations. I also had a group of sixth formers for the advance level Communication Studies Exam, which has a school-based assessment component. In addition, I was preparing a group, in the Evening School, to sit literature as a final exam. In addition, I was coaching the Debate Team. Since I am also an active Jehovah's Witness, I had to find time to prepare for and attend all my meetings, as well as participate in the preaching work.

With that schedule, I could not assist Mrs. Thompson, the coach of the quiz team, when I learned that she needed help. I could not find even a half-an-hour after school to help. She also expressed concern over the fact that they did not have anywhere to practice as a team as the dorm was not habitable. I had an extra room that was unoccupied. I told her if she could get another mattress, they could use the room. Problem fixed.

Helen Keller said that the highest result of education is tolerance. There is no way in life that you can live in a house with four teen age boys and maintain all your sanity. Some of my friends may query whether I managed to retain mine, but I am not asking them. These boys were from different backgrounds. Much credit goes to their parents and guardians. They were mature and disciplined young men. When there was any cause for concern, I would bring it to their attention and they would often make the needed adjustment. The fact that I had taught them years before was helpful. They still had that dread of incurring my displeasure thus keeping intact their wholesome respect.

There was one messy problem that had the potential to be hair raising, but this was soon put to rest with a little sense of humor.

I had spoken to them several times about washing the grease ring from the bath when they were through. One evening I went in the bathroom and was greeted by the unpleasant sight again. There was one among them who was the leader. He was known for his preaching, which resulted in him being dubbed the school's chaplain. The others respected him; he prayed with them morning and night. I thought it was a good idea to bring the problem to his attention since all my other efforts had failed.

"Delgado, look at this," I said indicating the scum in the bath, "I've spoken to you guys about this many times before. It's really unloving to the other users of the bath and it is unhygienic. Man, I can soon tell who just bathed by the hairs remaining."

His reply didn't miss a beat.

"Ooh yes! By their fruits you shall know them."

It was terse and in a tone that would cause old women in the back of the church to cry, "Amen!" I still chuckle at the memory. For that period there was no escaping school. It was eight to seven each evening except Tuesdays and Thursdays when I went to the Kingdom Hall, and Fridays when I relaxed and put my feet up and let my hair down, as the saying goes. The need for a real break was fast approaching; I could feel it lapping at me as my desire for change rolled in like waves being pushed by a stiff breeze.

CHAPTER THREE

Time for a Change: The Push Factors

"Y'u sure Mardri? Y'u sure 'bout dis? Make sure you know. Member, you have a permanent position here and dose tings don't always work out."

This was my friend Tac. I call her Tac, but she doesn't know that I do. It's an appropriate name because it is the initial letter of each of her names and most significantly, it characterizes her. Like a tack, she is as tough as nails; she can hold things together or change course suddenly. She can be prickly like a tack or tactless at times, but I love her and value her opinions because when we talk I'm forced to examine my own arguments. She has her own views and is in the habit of voicing them quite forcibly. After a long and mentally exhausting discussion, I usually arrive at a conclusion sometimes in difference, but well-thought-out because of Tac's tenacity and, sometimes, the insightfulness of her arguments.

There she was asking me whether I was sure. Sure? The word echoed through my mind. Are you sure, you sure—u sure? No! I was not sure. Who can be sure of anything? Teaching overseas offered no real guarantees. It was one of those cases where you would take a leap of faith. It was a risk and life was full of risks. Everything we do, we are taking a risk. Even if you don't take a risk, you have taken a risk. To answer her question I said, "Well, it's something I'd like to do. You know I came to this school five years as a student, go college an' been teaching here eleven years now. Man, we need to get away sometimes. All my qualifications are here in Jamaica. I tell you somting, every teacher should take a break from their situation every now and again. It should be mandatory."

"A true, you know, gal." With that she belted out one of her healthy belly laughs. I could see that she was turning over the idea in her mind.

I had to survive arguments with her a few years before, when I decided to go to university. The truth is I had to go some place at the time, any place. There was a situation that was threatening my spirituality and sometimes the best way to survive is to move from the danger zone. Although she was unaware of the push factor at the time, the reasons I presented were logical, true and valid; and they were accepted.

On the matter of my decision to go abroad to study and teach, she went on to remind me of the situation in which I had found myself. Some staff members thought I had been slighted when I was passed over for an appointment to senior teacher. I will call it an incident with which I had become uncomfortable.

Initially, I was not sure what had happened. The first staff member to approach me on the matter had asked, "Ms. Margery…" (I felt old when she said that, but she was an older woman and I'd like to think it was her way of being respectful.) "…Ms. Margery, how long you teaching here now?"

"Twelve years."

"You a Senior Teacher?"

"No?" I was wondering what this interrogation was about, but decided to go with it for awhile.

"Jesus— wid all a wha' yu do in dis place here? I tell you—yu see… The people in this place not easy yu know—dem not easy at all!"

She was obviously indignant about something, but what?

"What you talking 'bout?"

"You did know dat dey gi' e Mrs. Mullings Senior Teacher position?"

"Yes. She told me." So this is the problem?

"An' you no say not'ing?" What could I have said?

"What can I say? She has been a teacher longer than me and she was a Senior Teacher at the school she's coming from."

"Top you damn fool missis—dat no have anything to do wid it! She wasn't here all dis time and Senior Teacher is not transferable. Moreover, look how much you do! You work very hard in this place… Boy – oh boy! Make me shut me mout." And with that she had shut her mouth. Not another word to me on the subject. But the news was getting around and other teachers were coming up to me trying to suggest that it was an act of injustice, a cause for offence.

While I could rationalize the rightfulness of the promotion, I must confess that I was disgruntled when the person in question had come to me later and said, "Oh, the Debate Club is in my job description."

That one really got me. It was my pet project. I had spent hours on line, in libraries, taking students to libraries as many as twenty miles away on a Sunday, taking students to workshops and matches from city to city, spending time after school to help with speech writing, preparation and rehearsals . After a few days of fending off the comments and seeing that I was still disgruntled, I approached her and told her how I felt.

"You know, with all of what is going on, I was fine. But there is something that really get to me. Other than the obvious underhanded way that a lot of the things went down, I can't understand why the principal would give you the Debate Club without saying anything to me when I have been running it successfully since my return from UWI."

"No, no. I said she told me to help you with the Club."

Yea, yea, yea – right! I thought. This was not worth the fight. After all, I had already made up my mind to leave. There was no point in fighting for something I didn't plan to keep. Not this time. I saw the students through the other matches. I let go of the reins by initiating the transfer. I had another teacher accompany the students to the final matches and encouraged her to work along with the new appointee. Students' minds are not a pawn in the Monopoly game.

My hackles were soon up again; the same person, a different position. The Head of the English Department had asked me to sit in on the Panel of Internal Evaluators as his representative. Incidentally, he had told me he was not consulted in the case of the appointment and had been very clear that he thought the process was unfair. I must hasten to add that this was a voluntary confession and that it had no bearing on the task I would perform.

The principal, another teacher and I went to the classroom. At the end of the lesson, we met in her office in order to discuss our observations and to coordinate our findings, so as to produce a final document based on the instrument from the Ministry of Education. That went relatively smoothly, except for a few areas of discrepancies which we eventually managed to settle.

I was flabbergasted when the principal turned to me and asked: "What do you think of Mrs. Mullings being made Head of Department?"

Was I hearing correctly? Will this thing never end?

The HOD had been teaching at our school for over twenty years. He had acted in the position of vice principal at least two times during my tenure. True, there were things he could do to have a more effective department. But which department couldn't use some improvement? I couldn't imagine what it would do to him if he were to be removed from the position. While I had no objection to Mrs. Mullings' upward mobility and forging ahead, I was concerned about the people in her wake. I tentatively asked the principal the burning question in my mind, "So, what will happen to Mr. Khan?"

"Oh, we'll find a position for him. We'll put him in charge of the Examination Center…"

Now you do understand why I regard the system as being ungrateful, disregarding and unrewarding. My sense of integrity dictates that I give my job my best. However, I am always conscious that my eternal future does not depend on it; neither should I expect it to be my sole source of happiness and fulfillment. Teachers are not indispensable and they are losing their value and their usefulness in this disposable society.

Before you bring in the verdict for or against the administration, there is a vital piece of evidence that should be presented. It may incriminate me, but you decide. Tac thought that what I did may have incurred the displeasure of those in command and maybe the reason, it appeared, that I had lost favor.

Unlike most schools overseas, in Jamaican high schools, it is the teacher who moves from one class to another, not the students. There is a central staffroom where the teachers have desks or cubicles. The students will move for vocational subjects and some other practical areas.

Our school has several buildings with the tallest having three floors. I had a class on all three—grade eleven at the top; ten in the middle; and nine on the ground floor.

One day I was in the middle of teaching a literature lesson in a grade nine classroom in the middle of the ground floor. First, I became aware of an eerie feeling. Initially, I was enveloped in hot air. There was a little breeze and the heat seemed to be coming in on it. Closely following that was a most pungent odor. I tried to stop my breath, but to no avail. It was as though I could have reached out and touched it. Never before did an odor seem so palpable. I gagged then coughed as the smell waft its way across the classroom and down my throat. When I recovered sufficiently from choking, I walked to the window from which the stench emanated and was forced to recoil.

The students were fanning themselves and accusing each other of being the source of the smell. I made another valiant attempt to look through the slits created by the slabs in the window slots. I was shocked! There was garbage of every description: drink boxes, foam cups and lunch boxes, plastics, papers, cans, food particles and other trash. These were lodged among over grown grass and brush wood. Because it had rained the day before, the odor was resurrected by the sun.

To cut this long story short, I'll skip to my decision. I discussed the problem with the students and pointed out the danger of this situation. I remind them of the report on the spread of diseases by mosquitoes, flies and rats. Since they were responsible for the accumulation of the "dump site," it was only fair that they should clean it. I spoke to the students on all three floors. I pointed out that I did not wish to aggravate them, but to agitate them. Yes, I wanted them to be agitated. It was sad that these young people were so comfortable in such an environment. These are the same people who will go on a bus to a beach somewhere to clean it up as a show. However, they had no qualm about polluting their environment.

They were given an ultimatum—I would not return to class until the area was clean. I told all the students who would be affected, the principal, the vice principals, guidance department and the staff. I went to the other classes on the other blocks, but not those involved. Nobody said anything to me except two teachers who asked me if I was really serious about not going back to class until the area was cleaned up. I sat at my desk and read SBA and graded portfolios.

Two weeks later we were finally provided with some large trash bags, soap and gloves. I insisted that the students, and not the ancillary staff, should clean the area. Accompanied by the principal, the dean of discipline, some students' representatives and a VP, we headed behind the building with the students from the respective floors. They complained initially, but as they worked and sweated they began to berate any and everybody who ever threw anything through those window slits and those who might do so in the future. When we stopped, in less than thirty minutes, they had collected thirty bags full of garbage! I reasoned that, since they had thrown it there, it was only fair that they should pick it up. Nobody from the administration said anything to me.

I hope that they learned from the experience, because I did. It was after that that I felt the temperature shifted to cold. The easy smiles had become a stiff baring of the teeth and the shoulders I wanted to lean on were cold. But students are at school to learn. They need to know how to care for and maintain the environment; it is their inheritance.

It's ironic that every morning in the National Pledge they say they would do just that; use the strength and vigor of their body in the service of their fellow citizens. The truth is, I don't say the pledge because I live by the Golden Rule and my allegiance is to God. I love God, my neighbors and myself, so I will not do anything knowingly that will adversely affect any in my love triangle.

If we are to believe the Chinese proverb, culture is a treasure which follows its owner everywhere. I hope that these students will develop a culture of respect for themselves, others and the environment and that they would abound in it as they grow older.

Tac did have a point. They could have been upset by my actions. I should not have had to make that call and when I did, if it was the wrong action, someone should have said something. I was not going to waste valuable time and energy on this cultural quagmire. I refused to be bogged down by such narrow mindedness and vindictive nature. I was about to soar above all that. It was time I moved on.

CHAPTER FOUR

Jamaica: Evaluations, Conflicts and Resolutions

I cherish the view that you can't improve when you are learning only from yourself. People often fall into a mode of complacency when they have nothing to aspire to. This is especially true when you lack that quality of being true to yourself. Most of my students have heard me say many times that I don't obey laws out of fear of punishment or a penalty. I obey because I see the wisdom and benefits in obedience. I clean under my bed, not because I expect someone to look under there, but because I know it is the right thing to do. This system of beliefs is transferred to teaching. If I were to prepare and teach well only when I expect a visitor, then both my students and I would be in a woeful state. As a result, when visitors arrive I am usually ready.

There are many instances in my career when I have reason to be pleased that I live by this simple rule. Often when our work comes under scrutiny, we may try to rise to the occasion. Some people may pull off a good first impression successfully; others may fail miserably. If, however, you have a good record of hitting the mark, always pulling out the stops, maintaining a high standard at all times—then you have nothing to fear. You have nothing to fear in an organization that has fair, unbiased personnel, one that can recognize excellence and supports the consistent development of such. This point can neither be overstated nor overrated. Before long you will appreciate that this is a crucial requirement to the effective operation of any successful business and it is especially true if the business is education.

As teachers we were used to internal assessment from the principal, an independent observer and a teacher of our choice. I was not aware that the Ministry of Education sometimes assessed the whole school. The first time I heard the term "empanelling" was in 1996. In the beginning I thought it was something to do with impeaching because of the fear that had gripped everyone. There was never a time like that before, that I can remember seeing the whole school work together with such gusto. Everybody was writing lesson plans and bringing books up to date. Teachers went to class on time and were always present. Students were nowhere on the corridors. Everyone was trying to convey the impression that we were a well-oiled machine that ran smoothly from regular maintenance and proper usage. We put our best on display. The whole plant was under the microscope. While some cracks, scratches and dirt came to the fore, they did not lack the sparkle, sheen and constant hum of activity.

Many of us had been lulling into a state of complacency, doing just enough to get by. We did our jobs, but our spirits were flagging from a feeling of being battered, demoralized and demotivated. The Ministry of Education was checking to see whether we were asleep at the wheel and inadvertently gave us a jolt. Most of us were reenergized. We sought to recapture that zeal we had at the beginning. Although the Ministry did not visit every teacher, we were all affected by the new mood.

Mrs. Archer, a lecturer from one of the local teachers' colleges, was the member of the panel who visited my class. She sat in the class, checked the students' work books, and read my feedback to them. She pointed out an error in one student's book that she thought I had overlooked.

I liked her approach: she had taken the piece, made a note, then brought it to my attention.

I explained that I was observing the work for another skill and that I was encouraged to focus on the skill being taught at the time, so as not to frustrate the students with too many corrections. She had a good suggestion. Her solution was that I could do both—not encourage and frustrate, but make a note of the common errors and discuss those as a class after returning the books. I would also continue to give attention to the particular skill being developed, that way they could make corrections while learning to master the new skill being taught.

Beyond that, she went on to tell me how impressed she was by the activities that the students were engaged with and went on to add that the quality of my teaching was at a high level. "Have you done your degree?" she enquired.

"No, I plan to do it soon."

"Well, Miss Wright, I'm very impressed. You are teaching at a high level. Those activities will serve them well later."

"Thank you," I beamed. It is always good to receive positive feedback.

"I wish you all the best. Have a good day."

"Thank you and same to you."

She had stopped by later to return my lesson plan book. Except for a few evaluations of lessons taught, all was in order.

My second assessment by the Ministry came when I was in the art department. I had returned from vacation and they were experiencing difficulty in finding an art teacher. Since there was a teacher in for English, I offered to teach art for the term. The principal was skeptical at first, but consented after he realized he had very little chance of sourcing an art teacher at such short notice and for such a short period.

Art was my first love. I did Physical Education because the College had reneged. They had told me at the interview that they were offering Art, but when I registered, it was off the table. Undeterred I threw myself in the program as I sought to attain my diploma in secondary education, majoring in English, with Physical Education as my option and complementing Social Studies.

Since I had a distinction in Art at the GCSE Ordinary Level and I had received an award for outstanding performance in the subject when I graduated from this very school, I was confident that I could teach it. After leaving school I had continued to hone my artistic abilities to the point that I was even able to sell a few pieces of work. Teaching Art would be a chance to fulfill a dream.

The short stint in the Art Department would prove to be a transformation and a relief for all concerned. At the time, the two female teachers of Art were off on study leave. The Head of Art Department was a renegade. He had taught me art as a student and the one other Art teacher, Paul, was his past student as well as mine. Paul was in the first batch of students I taught in 1994 when I just started to teach. I taught him English or, as he would tell you, I tried to teach him English. He began working as a pre-trained teacher shortly after graduation. It was very difficult to get trained Art teachers in the rural parts of the island. Many stay in the city after they finished their training, while others branch out in the private sector, which is usually more lucrative.

The HOD, Mr. Hilton, was a renegade. He was famous for his liaisons with the female students, as well as his use of alcohol, marijuana and cigarettes, among other things. Members of staff, the student body and the community were puzzled about his continued presence on the campus, where he also lived and his position in the teaching profession—in spite of all the delinquency on his part.

All this climaxed during my time in the Art department. Mr. Hilton was declining in popularity and in morals—if the latter was possible—and he was not handling it well. The girl he was going around with at the time had just graduated. There were rumors that another student, one from the current batch, was not alone in her body thanks to him. He was hardly at school, although he lived on campus. His nefarious life style had escalated and he was not receiving much work on the side.

Teachers in the Visual Art and Industrial Art departments often moonlight by taking on jobs in their skill area in order to augment their salaries. Mr. Hilton was famous for his skill as an artist and for his ability to find people to get the job done. Recently he had been losing jobs, because it was apparent he was not meeting deadlines. Those who worked with him had been given cause to complain and had left him as a result. Both new and former clients were now turning to Paul, his former student. Mr. Hilton was not happy.

The tension was building. Both he and Paul were preparing students to sit the Art and Craft Examination at the Caribbean Examination Council. They had been working on the School Based Assessment section for weeks. After school, Paul would work on the jobs he was doing on the side. These involved t-shirt printing, making banners, posters among other things. In addition, he was creating pieces to build his portfolio, since he was finally determined to go to the Edna Manley School of Arts.

One morning Mr. Hilton came to the office I was using. After a brief greeting he wasted no time in getting to the matter that was of serious concern to him.

"You can teach C.X.C Arta?" he asked, with a slight lisp and his usual echo at the end of his sentence.

"No, sir. You know is English and P.E. me train to teach." We often resort to using Jamaican Creole when we are not in a formal setting or if the first speaker has set the tone by speaking Jamaican even in a formal situation.

"A-Oha. Bu' it not 'ard. You could a teach it wid ease… Dat bowai afi lef dis place. 'im a dis mana. Any 'ow you wi' 'ear wha' a go 'appen ova deh tidaya!"

"A which boy you mean?" I enquired, trying to learn why he was so upset. I suspected what the problem was.

"No' de one Paul? 'im ca' tan ya!"

With that declaration, he slammed his smoke-blackened fingers on the table for emphasis, and then he wheeled and left the room. The cigarette smoke and sweat lingered as a reminder that he had been in my room, long after he had left. I went to warn Paul that Mr. Hilton was around and that he was in a foul mood.

Paul merely laughed, hissed his teeth and said, "Cho! Dat a idiot!" He smiled this time, shook his head and sauntered off to his classroom.

Did you ever notice how these self-assured men move as though they were never in a hurry? He had every reason to feel confident. He is a well-built young man. Although I would not build a show down between himself and Mr. Hilton as a Fido Dido vs. Hulk, it would be a fair comparison. It would be something like a fly and heavy weight in the boxing ring.

When I heard the banging and shouts, I ignored it, initially thinking it was just the students at it again, being disruptive. You can never be sure if they are simply happy or very frightened. It soon became clear that the desperate screams were from girls in the other classroom down the hall. I rushed out of my office. I tried to make sense of what I was seeing. A girl was cowering against a wall, her face was red and tears streamed down her cheeks. She was clutching the piece of cloth she was preparing for batik in her printing project. Across from her, two others were clinging together. The boys stood by helplessly and all eyes were strained in the direction of Paul's office. I could hear muffled sounds coming from the office and the banging was still in progress.

The girls all turned to me and started gibbering in unison. I was moving toward them when Mr. Hilton emerged from Paul's office. He was panting and remonstrating as he left. "Yu afi know say yu caa' especk' fi dis man an' get 'way wid ita. Yu 'ear dat punku? Yu done know say dat caa' worko!"

When he saw me, he turned. Paul was rounding the corner toward me. He seemed ruffled. There were bruises on his body which were already rising. He too was breathless. Simultaneously, they started to recount what had happened. Paul had hardly opened his mouth when Mr. Hilton picked up a piece of aluminum, used as straight edge in art class. It was about three inches broad by approximately four feet long. He was determined to do harm with it. Paul held up his hand to protect his head as blows rained on him. He grabbed the weapon, but was ineffective as it hit the roof then the wall. Mr. Hilton had gotten hold of another object and they raced toward me trading blows like swords men in a duel or two men in a fencing match. Paul lost his weapon and he sped toward the door with Mr. Hilton on his heels. They were caught in the doorway. Paul reached down and picked up a wooden stool with metal legs and crashed it against Mr. Hilton's head. He collapsed to the floor unconscious.

The boys rushed to him and turned him over. They used a book to fan his face. When there was sign of life, they helped him to his feet and walked him around. He was limp and his voice was barely audible.

By this time, Paul had jumped over the side rails and had landed downstairs, thankfully, with all his bones intact. He ran to the main office, called the police and reported the incident to the Principal. The students led Mr. Hilton downstairs and I tried to comfort the girls and to answer the telephone. Everyone wanted to know if I was fine. I learned a long time ago how to conduct myself in a fight that I was not a part of. My brothers taught me well. "Cockroach no business in a fowl fight." In spite of this, I was quite shaken up inside.

I had to prepare statements for the Principal and the Police. The stool was confiscated. Both men were suspended and the Art Block was a lonely place. There were stories all over the school and the community about what had happened. I tried as best as I could to hold things together.

Only Paul returned. Mr. Hilton was given the option of resigning. He took it. He was finally gone. What a way to go!

Paul and I were the only two present when the assessors came. By that time, he was healing slowly, but was still in pain. The representative from the Ministry spent some time with us. He did not have a chance to see us teach, but he looked at my plans and examined the students' work. We discussed the goals of the department and shared ideas that could improve it and make it more visible in the school.

He thought I was an asset to the department. He pointed out that since I was acting in the capacity of the senior teacher, I should receive an increase in my salary. I would later receive an increment for protective clothing after I brought this knowledge to their attention. The experience was beneficial. I got valuable experience and my confidence grew.

The third time around was under challenging, but less dramatic circumstances. This was after I had returned from university. As students, we had been given the task to evaluate the Reform of Secondary Education Curriculum (ROSE). We were encouraged to use the approach set out in this instrument when we went back to our schools. It meant using a thematic approach from grades seven to nine, in our attempt to develop students' language skills and to enable them to be more language aware. I grew to value the approach and to adopt it in teaching language arts to the only grade nine that I was teaching English language arts that year. I taught the other grade nines literature.

This method incorporated the other subject areas. In itself, this was an advantage to all concerned. I could use the vocabulary from other subjects in the language class. In this way the words would be common and meaningful to the students as they are not learning in a vacuum. They see how learning these content areas become relevant in the world in which they live and operate. When for example, we were working on the theme of "The Environment and You", we worked closely with the Science department. Students who were exploring noise pollution could use their science textbooks for materials. They had to get content for their speech or presentation about the cause and effect of noise pollution. Mrs. Morgan, the Biology teacher, was kind enough to grade the diagrams of the ear. She was able to have me help her reinforce the technique for drawing diagrams for the purpose of Science which is different from that of Art.

In spite of my efforts, the students were most unhappy. They wanted to be doing what the other students were doing. I have always felt that students are younger and sometimes smaller people. They deserve to be treated respectfully and they should be allowed to express themselves respectfully and freely without any threats of reprisals. There are times I will not like what I hear, but if I am mature then I should be able to handle the matter in the right spirit. At the same time, there are other issues that may demand that the teacher lay down the rules and there is no room for arguments. On this matter though, I thought that an open discussion could settle the matter.

"OK. There is no question you're upset. Here is the situation, I want you to select someone from among you, who you are sure understands the problem and can explain it clearly. Starting now, you have five minutes to select your spokes person."

They agreed to this and set about their business. Janel was appointed. She was articulate and apparently fearless. I liked her because she displayed great leadership potential and I was sure she would have a brilliant future if she learned to control her natural abilities.

"Miss, my classmates and I believe that we are not being given a fair chance to learn. We are not doing the same things as the other students in grade nine. We want to do well in our exams and it is not right that the teacher is not doing what she is supposed to do and teach us."

"Yes."

"Is true dat!"

"Bap—bap!" the others would chime in each time they heard something that they agreed with. She looked at them and they would become quiet, but would hold up their thumb, nodded or displayed some other symbol of support.

When she was finished I asked that I be allowed to respond. "What do you think you should be learning in this class?" It was best to try reasoning with them.

"Well, we should be learning to write sentences, compositions, we should learn about verbs and nouns and do comprehension and tings like dat." This brought with it a round of applause.

"Please tell me this: what did you learn to do in grade three?"

"We learned to spell, and read, and write and to say poems."

"Did you learn about the parts of the sentences and how to use the different parts of speech?"

"Yes, Miss!" That was the whole class.

"And you learned that in grades four, five and six. Then you came to high school. Now tell me: what did you learn in grade seven?"

"We did fill-in-the-blanks and composition and comprehension and letter writing and poetry." They seemed very pleased as the list was being reeled off.

"Didn't you do these things in grade three as well?"

"Yes Miss, but it's different. It's not the same thing."

"You need to remember that learning is a process. The things you were learning in those early stages were skills you need to operate at this level. Having mastered those skills, you need now to use them in the wider society. What you are now leaning to do is to apply those skills to the real world. The ROSE curriculum will allow you to use these language skills you have been learning. It helps you to become more aware of your environment and gives you the language skills to master it."

"A true you know."

"Dat make sense Miss."

"Den why make the odder pickny dem not doing it and de odder teacha dem not doing it needa?" There is always a dissenting voice the doubtful Thomas among us. These were valid questions, but the speaker was using this line of reasoning to justify not doing the things we were doing.

"Here's what I would suggest you do. Think seriously about what we have been doing. As we do these different topics, do you write compositions, letters, write creative sentences, learn new words and how to use them correctly?"

"Yes, Miss! Like how we write about the different types of pollution, and the effect, and write a letter to our neighbor about the loud music and the pig pen stinking up the place..." The others laughed.

"Miss, I get what you saying now. We doing every ting we should be doing and more. So we doing more dan de oder children dem." Thanks for the bright spark. She must be good at math. Having added everything she came up with a good conclusion.

"So, Miss, why the other children not doing the same thing?"

"Ehee! What make dem not doing it too?"

"I am not quite sure. I am going to suggest that if you still have doubts about this matter then you go and speak to the Principal. I have spoken to her about what we are doing and she would be more than pleased to answer any question you might have. May I continue the class now?"

"Yes, Miss!" With that, they took out their books and were ready again for that day.

Not many days after this they were back to the beginning. The situation reminded me of the Israelites coming from the land of Egypt. It only takes a few complainers, usually the ones who have no interest in it either way. They start murmuring and the whole class gets it. That's how a good thing suddenly goes south.

One day they went overboard. This time I had to get the message across to them that their conduct was unacceptable and that I would not tolerate that kind of behavior. I liked the fact that as teacher I had some amount of autonomy and did not have to go to the office except as a last resort. When the children refused to settle down, I decided to wait on them. Instead of getting quiet as is customary, they broke out in songs. There were several students in the class who were also members of the school's choir and the others had no problems in joining the impromptu chorale. Before I knew what was happening, they had caught a tune and were keeping it alive as they sang and clapped and rocked. They sang many of the popular songs that spoke to oppression and injustice. They made changes where they could to make the songs relevant.

"Longing for—what are we longing for—for Miss Wright to release the door."

That was based on one song by an entertainer who was singing while still in prison yearning to be released. The second one had to do with the fact that it was lunch break and we were still in the classroom. There was no point in shouting at them. I was holding the handle or the trigger. They were holding the wrong end. I would wait. I would hold my tongue. I would make them see. For now they sang on…

"Prison life it no sweet
For right here now we no have noting to eat…"

They sang and laughed and I made notes as I stood and waited. This was a mind game. They always break. Sometimes as teachers, we make the mistake of giving them a piece of our minds. If we do, we may lose everything. When students are on the war path, it is all or nothing. But, when I am not getting angry and I am calm, they are confused. When they are exhausted from pushing my buttons and I refuse to start, they become quiet, then they turn on each other. They become divided and, as you know, if they are divided, they will fall.

First, they curse at me- they come to school to learn and teachers not teaching them and they don't think that it is fair because they pay their school fee and teachers suppose to teach and they are going to the office because nobody should mess with their future and they go on and on…

Genuine students are usually honest. They would admit that their behavior was not conducive to learning. On this day in question, it was Oshane who lashed out. I can't remember if he was among those singing with the others, but it took all of them by surprise when he began to speak.

"De whole a unu betta shut unu mout. Look how long de woman a try fi teach an unu won' tap chat. Look how long him a wait pon unu, an unu di deh a disrespeck him. All you…"

By this time he was crying as he reprimanded and rebuked. Except for his broken voice and his sniffles—there was silence in the classroom—no singing, no cursing, and no moving. All eyes were turned on him in the corner near the back of the class where he was standing.

He called out each of the instigators and he quoted them on what they had said and pointed out to them the duplicity in their claims, the way their conduct conflicted with their lines of arguments. I was proud of him. I could not have said it better myself.

The teacher for the afternoon session arrived and I left. I reported the incident to the Form Teacher and the Vice Principal. I asked for permission to invite the parents and guardians to the school so that I could make them aware of what had been happening. I wanted them to be aware of what I was trying to do and to get them to help their charges to make the needed adjustment so that we could proceed in an orderly fashion. Surprisingly, the resistance did not come from the parents, but from a teacher. Her response came after she had spoken to the students.

"You can stay dere a play hero. Me?" she said slapping her chest with her open palm. "Me naa play no hero!"

With that she laughed and walked away. That was just another hazard in the workplace. In the teaching profession too often you don't get the support when you need it. True, we don't want a "we against them" situation, but students need to know that the staff is operating as a unit, that we have the same objective—attaining their best interests.

My third assessment from the Ministry of Education came in the middle of all of this conflict. In my view it could not have been at a more suitable time. No, I don't think I was the only person who was glad to see them. I was especially pleased because I learned that one Dr. Wright was on the panel and that he had worked on a team at the Ministry that was spearheading the drive to have the ROSE Curriculum implemented.

After he had evaluated me teaching my grade ten English class, I invited him to visit my grade nine language arts class and to speak to them about the thrust of the Ministry to have educators using the approach to help students to master the skills in language acquisition.

I had gotten to the classroom ahead of him, so I had enough time to inform the students of his pending arrival and what he purposed to do. It is the custom that when a teacher enters the classroom the students stand; I always try to get through this greeting quickly so that the squeaking, screeching of desk and chairs can end. This is the concert segment.

"Good afternoon, everyone!"

"Good afternoon, Miss Wright!" they chorused.

"Please be seated."

I resisted the urge to use my fingers to stop my ears. Thankfully, they settled down quickly. Since I was not sure when Dr. Wright would arrive, I started the class after reminding them that we were expecting a visitor.

When he arrived they did their usual greeting. There was no doubt that they were trying hard to impress him. Just to look at them—they all looked as though they could not mash an ant. Who would think that they were capable of such riot or of being the bane of my very existence at times? First, the cacophony of the desk, chairs and children's voices commingled, and then there was silence. I decided to do the introduction and to get this thing underway.

"You'll remember I told you that someone from the Ministry would come to speak to you about that concern you have and the things we have been doing in class. Today we have Dr. Wright with us——" I was cut short.

"Miss, is you bredda?"

"No, we are not related—it's just a name incident." When the laughter died down, I continued. "Now, we have had some long discussions, you and I, and I really want to set your hearts at rest, so don't be afraid to ask Dr. Wright whatever you want to know about this issue." Turning to him, I said. "Sir, I know you're busy so I will turn them over to you."

He thanked me, then made a few opening remarks. He asked them to tell him what they had been learning in class. They told him and I found my head growing in spite of myself. Sometimes you don't realize how much you have taught or how much the students have learned until some moments like this. He basically connected the dots and reinforced the importance of what the Ministry is trying to do in this approach to teaching and learning. The students seemed reassured, I felt reaffirmed and he told them what he thought of me as a teacher. If you see my head seems a little big, it is because of all those wonderful things he said about my teaching. After this he had asked me when did I plan to move on to teach at the college level and encouraged me to give it serious consideration.

That was not to be the end of the testing for me. There was an old man on the panel. He had a most eccentric appearance. He was rotund with a red, green and gold knitted tam perched precariously on the top of his head. He reminded me of those pictures of the old Chinese men in their pajama-style pants with suspenders. This one had come out of retirement and out of the woodworks for the occasion. Do you want to know the truth? I didn't want him to see me. There were horrible stories going around that he was disagreeable, hypercritical and impossible to please. Apparently, Dr. Wright had told him of our encounter during one of their meetings and he wanted to see me himself. He told me he would be there and I went to class with great trepidation.

We were not going to do anything special for the occasion. It would be business as usual. The students were placed in groups for the presentation of a poem. The title of the poem is *Darkie Sunday School*. They were given the latitude to employ different genre to make the presentation creative. This was one method of engaging students. These classes would average forty students so it was not always possible to grade students' work individually or read each piece all the time. You soon learned to use creative means to evaluate and assess. I was also cognizant of the fact that students learn in different ways. It is natural that they should be evaluated in varied ways too.

Each group was given the guidelines against which the presentation would be judged. They would be watching for creativity, audibility, clarity and originality. Since they were made aware of the importance of pitch, pace and power in order to convey the mood and tone, they were ready to perform and judge. I gave them the score sheets and they were ready.

Each group would pay close attention to the performances, assign number grades as suggested on the grade sheet, discuss the areas of strength and weakness, select a group representative to read their score and announce the group's conclusion.

In terms of creativity, they could sing, read, rap, preach, make a speech, act, mime, narrate or any media or genre they could use effectively to relate the account of the poem, *Darkie Sunday School*. They were also encouraged to use props and to dress the part. We had gone over the rules and they would see me on the corridors and tell me to expect to be entertained—and I was looking forward to be amazed. I told them they could borrow the drums and sticks that are kept in the staffroom.

I got to the classroom early and our visitor was right there with me. There was no time to warn them or prepare them so I told them who he was and explained what we were going to do—as if they needed any reminder. Because of the visitor they were timid at first. After a shaky start, the show was underway. The group that was to go first was making excuses, but when I threatened not to let them go at all, they got to the front of the class and did their thing.

Usually I position myself at the back of the class for oral presentation. This gives me a full view of the other students and it forces the presenters to project their voices so I can hear them because I am grading too. The visitor had taken a seat in the middle and the other students were sitting in their groups. The students got into gear and they made me proud. They employed all sorts of choral arrangements and many different artistic styles. At the end, that little man from the Ministry came to life. You would have thought that he was on Broadway.

"Bravo! Bravo!" he shouted, as he clapped gleefully.

Throughout the piece, he had applauded enthusiastically and laughed out loud in parts. At some points he forgot his role and doled out commendation and advice. We were all thoroughly entertained.

As we walked back to the staffroom, he could not contain himself. "Oh! Miss Wright, you have made my day. That was wonderful. For years I have been looking for this kind of teaching. I'm so pleased to see that there is still teaching in our schools. We want to see more of this in the classroom today. Yes! You have to capture the imagination of the students. So, what else have you been doing with them?"

"Well, I have some scrapbooks and projects in the staffroom. If you'd like, you may have a look."

I didn't want to tell him about the talk show we had where we discussed current topics for a few minutes each morning. Or the call-in programs, where students got to be radio moderators and others were concerned citizens calling in to share their views and concerns. These were models from the wider society. When we played at these games, students became more language aware and would switch their code and register depending on the role they were playing.

Since we were doing poetry, every type of poem that was taught, they also had to write one of their own. At that point, they had their own samples of haiku, limerick, sonnet and concrete or form poems. In addition to creating their own poems, they had to illustrate them by drawing and coloring or using pictures and different fonts. First, the poems were written and reviewed in class, which allowed me to see the progress and that they were doing their own work.

He leafed through some of the books "oh-ing and ah-ing" as he went. After reiterating how pleased he was, he left. The principal told me some time afterward that I had really made an impression on the panel.

This kind of feedback was very encouraging because many days I felt as if I were fighting a losing battle. Because literature was not offered as one of the subjects in the final exit exams, the school allowed students to do it from grade seven to grade nine. I was at liberty to explore the genre as I saw fit. Initially, I was the sole teacher of literature at grade nine, but when I was asked to teach Communication Studies, I asked to be relieved of some of the literature sessions. The other teacher and I worked closely together because I had to provide her with the syllabus and the content. This was crucial because all the students would be sitting the same end of term examination.

"Miss, a true dat de book boring?" one of the first questions I had to parry.

"Yes maama, mi hear say it long an boring. And it no have no picture?" Another student had provided a response.

"So, Miss, why we caan read interesting book in a class?"

This was really growing into a standoff. The complainers were warming up. I had to step in before it took root among them. There was nothing that could rob you of your joy and faith more quickly than a bunch of murmurers. I had to turn on the saleswoman part of me. I needed to convince them that literature was an exciting subject and that the text was a book that they would regret not reading all their lives if they missed out on this opportunity.

The sale of the course to the students involved some serious advertising. I had a brilliant idea and shared it with some other teachers, who then encouraged me to work on it. I had to get permission from the principal, so I went to her.

After we chatted for awhile I shared the idea. "I would really like to put on a literature exhibition to expose the students to the different works and some of the classics, as well as some Caribbean writers."

"That's a good idea, but how would you do it?"

"I could use that room that the student teachers use when they are here."

"You mean the Overseas Exam Room?"

"Yes. It is not being used now and I would like to keep the display in place for a couple weeks since some other teachers have expressed an interest in having their students view the exhibit."

"That's a very good idea. I'll ask Mrs. Taylor to get it ready. When did you say you want it for again?"

"The earlier the better because I need to do this before the students get their texts."

"Okay, I'll see to it."

"Thanks and I hope you'll get a chance to drop by."

"I'd like that."

I knew that this sort of thing would interest her because she had taught English when she was in the classroom. In fact, we would sometimes sit in her office and just talk about teaching. She taught me when I was in grade eleven and we sometimes compared teaching then and now, or simply revisited literary works we had read, studied or taught.

I raided my personal library at home, got permission to use some books from the school's library and Mrs. Lodge, the reading teacher, lent us a few. With the help of some sixth formers, I posted the charts I had made with the use of appropriate pictures from old calendars. My calligraphy skills kicked in as I wrote suitable and informative charts to explain the different types of books.

There were different types of novels, print and audio, anthologies, the complete works of Shakespeare, Caribbean writers, plays, music and movies. I especially wanted them to see the other works by the author that we would be studying in class. They met Emily Dickinson, Derek Walcott, Langston Hughes, Lorraine Hansberry and many more. There was a section labeled for each genre and samples of the works that were available.

Many of the books in the library had been removed over time. Some had been moved because of water damage after one hurricane; others because new books from HEART Trust NTA had been promised. When they received new books, from many different sources, including North Carolina, there was no librarian to catalogue them. Not surprisingly, many of these books went missing; whoever wanted them took them.

The different classes were taken in groups of fifteen until the entire class had seen it. The students had to write about their experience at the exhibition. Although many of them had been members of libraries at some point, they had never seen the literary works arranged in that particular order before. Most of them were pleased with the display and asked to borrow books. Some had read one book by an author and were interested to see that they had written other works and so they asked to borrow them. There was so much I wanted to expose them to, but it was difficult to take out such a large group and there was no literary exhibition that I was aware of. True, there was the Calabash Literary Festival, but it was more modern contemporary and it was staged in the holidays. I would encourage students to attend because there were Nobel laureates as well as other regional and foreign writers there; moreover, the festival was free.

When we started the text selected for the class, *Crick Crack Monkey,* written by Merle Hodge, we spent two sessions analyzing the blurb, then the symbols and images on the cover. We made predictions and they were raring to go. The text was right up their street. Since we were exploring the universal themes, I allowed the students to select appropriate songs that have similar themes. Because these singers and song writers were from different parts of the world, they could make general comments about how the issues cut across culture and other divides. At the same time, they were learning to use their abilities at different levels. They kept a scrapbook album of the characters. They could get pictures from the newspapers and magazines. They listened, analyzed and synthesized as they produced their own work to show how the issues appeared in their own experiences.

In order to make the story come alive for the students, I often tried to read in the tone or accent of the dialect in which the text was written. They loved it when I read the parts of Tantie, imitating the Trinidadian voice. They laughed and clamored for more. There was no problem with controlling their behavior. I merely had to threaten them with not reading or not allowing them to read and dramatize parts of the text. You have heard it said that there are many ways to use whipped cream? This was one sure way of getting them to sit attentively in class.

If I told you that they were all little angels, I would be lying. There was one class that I could not do much with in one way or the other. It was a large group of students and a large classroom. Many of these students were coming to the school for the first time in grade nine. A number of them were in some sporting activity, some of the girls were brassy and played soccer or netball. The boys were athletes, footballers or cricketers and, while they excelled in these areas, some found the academic tasks to be something of a challenge.

The location and appearance of the classroom did not help matters. It was toward the back of the school. Although the room was large and new, there was one door, as was the case with many of the others. In the previous year, one teacher was locked in that very room after she had confiscated something from a student. Another problem with that room was that the ceiling was low and leaked when it rained. The darkness was intensified by the fact that there were decorative blocks instead of windows, on the west side there were a few rows and the east side had a half-a-wall of blocks. The north wall was solid, but there were holes in the south wall where the teacher and the whiteboard stood and beyond that was another classroom. Try to imagine this setting after PE in the forty degrees heat of Santa Cruz, and then add the noise from next door. Imagine also a creepy crawly lizard innocently climbing through those blocks from the bushes beyond and you would have a vivid image of how forty-plus students can be transformed into a pack of one hundred hyenas. Believe me when I tell you that the very thought of going to that class left me drained.

As I got to know them, I realized that they weren't uncivil out of a desire to be mean; rather, they behaved in that way because they did not know better. They conducted themselves in that way out of habit. When some of the parents arrived for Parents' Day, they behaved the same way toward them and the parents found it acceptable. The children were unaware of any professional distance between adults or teachers and themselves, therefore, when I tried to remind them of this, they thought I was just being fussy and aloof.

Although they had many problems to contend with, it was amazing to see how these children loved and protected each other. There was a group of girls who behaved like mothers or leaders to the others. They spoke up for others, shared their lunches with those who didn't have, and kept tabs on each other. One morning I saw the group of girls bawling. They hugged each other and struggled to a bench half carrying one of their members. I moved toward them to find out what was the cause of this wailing.

"What's the matter?" I enquired, concerned that this should be going on especially with the others at assembly.

"Anna-Lisa gran-mada dead, Miss!" they chorused and the sobbing continued. I looked among them, but there was no sign of Anna-Lisa.

"I'm sorry to hear that. Where is Anna-Lisa?" They were at the bench outside a classroom some sitting others crowding around all crying.

"She gone home, Miss. Her auntie call her and tell her... Oh my—Miss is a nice lady, you know, she did really nice. Is she take care of Anna-Lisa..."

The speaker broke off and covered her face in her hand, bent forward and smothered her sobs in another girl's lap. As I watched them crying together, I was forced to realize once again, the power of the community and love. As a teacher I had learned to be patient and to understand how this unit operated in order to deal with them better. Ranting and punishing did very little for this group. They had a different way about them. Patience and reasonableness was the way to them. Although they were crude, I could not be crude enough to match them and I could not go low enough to shock them—not that I would want to. They responded to love and I was comfortable with love.

Another issue that had become a great cause for concern was the annual workshops. Let me admit to this fact: Repetition is essential in education. Life is impossible without repetition. We develop our wholesome routine and establish our rhythm based on repetition. It is variety that makes repetition bearable. Variation in time, amount and method are some areas that make repetition enjoyable. Workshops are arranged to help teachers to see how to create these varieties.

Teachers recognize the importance of attending workshops, staff development sessions and other ongoing training. Sometimes we become so comfortable in one cycle we are afraid to try new things and that is sad. That is defeating the whole purpose of education. As educators, we are obligated to teach others to think and when they have thought then they should apply what they have learned. There cannot be any true education without real and observable change. Since I live by this concept, you can perhaps imagine my disappointment with the majority of the workshops I have attended. My HOD, who had been teaching for over twenty years, had gotten in the habit of sending other teachers especially the younger and newer ones.

"Marj, you want to go? You go—I tiad a dem damn tings man. I does go and every time is the same ting dey doing. Dey all crazy!" he would say in his Guyanese lilt.

I went. I wanted to prove him wrong. At first, it was new and exciting. Maybe it was the fact that I was out of school for a day, it was something different. Then I thought that maybe they were expecting a new set of teachers each year. Therefore, they did not want to change anything. But these workshops were planned for teachers who were instructing senior students. It was natural to expect that most schools would retain their staff for the students sitting external examinations. Wouldn't it be fair to assume that some of the same teachers would turn out for the refresher course?

After awhile even the hotel accommodation lost its appeal. Yes, we would be hosted in style at hotels in different parts of the island; the city, or the North Coast, which is the tourist Mecca. It was not merely the content that was pedestrian, but the resource team was tired. When I started teaching in 1994, these women were the presenters. In 2006 and all the time in between, they were still presenting. While nothing is bad or wrong with that in itself, something must be wrong if they were using the same handouts and the same medium of presentation.

One year the presenter, who actually has a doctorate, changed some of her worksheets used as samples. This was compulsory as the format of the exam had changed and she was using that past paper to make her point. That was about all the changes though because we, the teachers in the group, had to explain to her the changes to the syllabus that had necessitated this adjustment in the exam format. This was news to her, I thought to myself,

If they have us, as a group, once per year and can't be more innovative, how can they be so critical of us who have to invent new ideas daily and weekly in order to keep students interested, motivated and actively involved?

This mental drought is taking place in a country with three major universities, several teacher training colleges and many secondary schools with a plethora of master teachers. Do you want to tell me that they could not find at least one new resource person each year? I like a stretch in my learning experience. Didn't these people have access to the internet and all those journals and magazines that show how the same old things can be taught using new methods?

At least the sole male presenter declared his hand early when he said, "I am a dinosaur. I have no cell phone, no microwave, not even an email address. Although I relented and bought a computer, it is just for the keyboard. My secretary refuses to use the old typewriter anymore."

With that he broke out in mock sobs at the memory of having surrendered in this one area to the progress of technology. He spoke with such pride and conviction; one was almost moved to commend him for being able to hold-out on technology.

There was a general feeling that they were not just tired, but bored with the task. They were well paid for each session which may have been the reason for prolonging the misery. I wouldn't ask someone to do something I was not willing to do myself. I also think that a person of integrity and excellence should realize when they are not doing justice to a job and leave it. If the delinquents are ignorant of their remission, the superiors should make them aware. When I can't change a situation I am in and I know that my charge or myself is being adversely affected, I ask for help. If the problem persists, I remove myself from the situation and see whether time can heal that wound. More often than not it works out for the good of all concerned.

CHAPTER FIVE

Surviving a Rigorous Recruitment Process

"Boy, oh boy— Marj, you no easy you know man. Girl, you good, you good, you good bad!"

Yes, that's a Jamaican for you; in one sentence you can have a woman who is a boy, a man and a girl. Liz was overwhelmed by my latest reaction to the bite of the travel bug. Liz, Tac and I had met in teachers' college. We had started working at the same school together. It was the first job for Liz and me. Tac had finished college a year before us. There was another first for us; we all went to Panama together. Liz and I were traveling for the first time and I have been traveling since. I had been telling her for some time that I wanted a change and finally the change was in progress.

"So Liz, you want to tell me that you never feel like you could take a break from all this? I mean, what's the point of being single, if we're just going to pass all our days in one place?"

"You can go on. I have no such aspirations. Mummy was telling me to go to Spain to teach English. Me?"

You'd have to hear her say that *me* to get the sense of her emotions. Me? It was loaded with "I wouldn't even consider such a notion!" No, that doesn't quite describe it. It was more a case of "me," as in, "You must be mad to think I would even consider such an idea!"

"But think, Liz, if you learned so much in Columbia in one month; imagine what you could accomplish in a year in Spain!" She is a teacher of Spanish and a very good one too, but she had made up her mind and she was not about to change it.

"No, sir, you can go on and tell me—me all right." was her respectful reply.

Now I was a man with a title. Yes, sir. Some people enjoy living vicariously. She was adamant that she was not hearing the call to serve abroad. What can I say, I tried. I was sharing my progress with her. She could provide feedback on some of the recruitment agencies. Another island would have been preferable, but I was yielding, under duress mind you, to go to the land where the greed was greater—if all else failed.

Because morale was low among the staff members, several members were seeking to make a move. Some desired to pursue their degree, others wanted to move up the corporate ladder and yet others merely wanted a change. This made it easy to get information on the viable recruiting agencies. Some of them did not have a very good reputation based on feedback from some who have been burnt, or those who have friends who have been dealt with unfairly by agents.

I started off with a list of five, including some other islands that were usually in the hunt for teachers. After my friends went through with the proverbial fine-tooth comb, I had two islands and two agencies and I expressed my interest in them. There was no response from the government, but the agencies responded. I decided to follow up on the one in the US, since I had already been to England twice. I wrote to thank the English Agents and promised that I would contact them in the near future. With that, I zeroed in on the US agency.

By December of 2006 I had gone online and had done my research. There were many local testimonies—but none was first hand or personal. There was an advertisement in the newspaper. I cut it out and filed it for future consultation. I completed the application, but did not submit it. They were not about to let me get off with that.

January 16, 2007
Thank You for Applying

Thank you, for beginning the_____ application process. We hope this leads you to a rewarding experience of teaching in the USA and sharing your personal and professional experiences as a cultural ambassador.

While you have started and saved your application online, your application has not yet been submitted___ for review...

You are encouraged to submit your completed application as soon as possible. The earlier we receive your application, the more opportunities you will have for a US teaching position next year...

Applying to the ___ Program is a commitment of time and energy and we appreciate your efforts as well as your interest.

I was about to see that the latter statement was no joke. This was another reason that caused Liz to think that I was "good bad." On top of my already crammed schedule of daily activities, I added an application process which was as intensive as a degree program. This process was complicated by the fact that it was the height of SBA grading and I had no internet access at home. It would have been good to simply get up and go online at nights after a few hours sleep. The truth is, I was not sleeping well because during the summer of the previous year, a burglar had come in the house one night while I was asleep and so I was sleeping fitfully ever since. Alas, internet access at home was not an option for me.

After I submitted the online application, the agency reviewed it and notified me of the telephone interview segment with my advisor. Each applicant is assigned an advisor.

The telephone interview was conducted between classes one day while I was in the staffroom. I could not find anywhere more conducive at the point, so I tried to make myself heard over the phone line above the din in the staffroom. I tried to speak above the animated chatter, which was customary there and yet maintain some privacy. There was never a more inconvenient setting, but I managed to convince the interviewer that she must find out more. Don't ask me what I said. I have very little memory of the details of that interview.

"Congratulations on your successful telephone interview. Now you should focus on the next steps in the admission process."

Steps indeed! Part one was more a case of verification of what had been done. They wanted the applicants to recheck and to ask any questions they may have as well as to add any necessary information.

Step two was the essay. This was to be completed before the personal interview. It was described as:

> *a crucial part of the process, as prospective US employers would review this essay before offering a teaching position. Warning: take this essay seriously and write the answer thoughtfully—your US adventure depends on it.*

The essay had to be on a successful lesson that I had taught. They expected to see what made it a success, how I catered to the students with varied abilities, and how the lesson objectives correlated with the curriculum. The essay should not exceed 5000 characters and it should be pasted in a given link-error free. The hardest part of this exercise was choosing the lesson—there were so many memorable lessons.

This is the essay that I wrote, describing my memorable lesson:

Memories of a Successful Lesson

"One test of the correctness of educational procedure is the happiness of the child."

Maria Montessori

Unquestionably, after eleven years in the classroom, there are many occasions that can be deemed

successful and memorable. There are some, however, that will stick with me for a very long time. A lesson I taught on the Simple Present Tense is a good example.

The Caribbean Examination Council's Chief Reporter had been complaining for some time about the weaknesses in students' narratives. He said that the stories lacked consistency in the use of tense and that the development failed to convey a sense of immediacy. It was clear that the students needed practice in this area. At the same time, teachers were being encouraged to move away from the "chalk and talk" and drilling exercises. The thrust was now towards practical lessons that students could relate to and apply on a daily basis. The lessons were to be made relevant to their lives.

Another crucial factor in the plan and execution of this lesson was the objectives of the Reform of Secondary Education Program. They (in the Ministry of Education) want to unify secondary education and to make it more effective and efficient. In this quest, both students and teachers seek to interact constructively with instructional material and equipment. This approach requires a cooperative learning environment which is child centered. It allows curiosity questioning, sharing and discussion which are prominent features in the learning process. Students are encouraged to realize their full potential through these methods.

This particular lesson was successful because the students were involved from the outset. After a quick revision of Subject and Verb Agreement, the lesson was underway. The students listened to the recording of the clip from the horse race commentary. They eagerly jotted down the verbs. During an animated discussion, they realized how the present tense was crucial to the excitement created in the account.

The same measure of enthusiasm was displayed in the other activities. These activities were appealing because majority of the students love sports. The clips were audio-visual and practical. Those who did not like sports were given a list of activities from which to choose. As a group, they presented a model contest with appropriate dress and music. Other members announced the models and described their attire.

This approach allowed all the students to participate. They were helped to be more sensitive to the value of language as a tool for expression, communication, learning and thinking. Students contributed in different skill areas based on their abilities. I was able to supervise seatwork and coax those who found the written work to be a challenge.

Those who shared their work did so willingly. The gleam in their eyes and their broad smiles were clear indications that they enjoyed the exercises. Weeks later they were still recalling snatches from that class. Their speech reflected an attempt to vary their verbs. The transition in their writing was slower and this timely change was understandable, as writing is not automatic. In spite of this, their effort was obvious and commendable.

As I taught, I was conscious of what Howard Gardner said, "…it is no longer a question of whether the students are intelligent but how are they intelligent?" The students were given the latitude to choose activities to complement their abilities. They worked well because the activities suited their abilities. They were motivated because the materials used were in their experience. They were happy. What more could a teacher ask for?

I also had to submit a lesson plan as well. They were really covering all the grounds. I liked that. So I really worked on that plan making sure I covered all the bases. I wanted it to be so detailed that someone could take it and teach from it, but that it would also reflect a realistic setting.

The lesson plan was designed for a class of grade nine students. The class consisted of forty-six students and the topic would be covered over four sessions or two hours and twenty minutes. We would work on the general topic of Tense with our focus on the Simple Present Tense.

You know as well as I do that learning does not take place in a vacuum. People can only learn something in relation to what they already know, that is how the brain works. It is a lot like building a house—it needs a base or foundation to stand on. The structure will not defy gravity and stand without the foundation in place. With this in mind, I started by establishing previous knowledge before taking them through the different uses and the effect of the Simple Present Tense. The time was enough to teach the concept and allow the students to carry out the activities to demonstrate mastery.

Step three of the application process involved another important task—the gathering of required documents. This was done over a period of several weeks, thousands of dollars, journeys into the city to see about my transcripts, the police record, and several telephone calls to follow up applications in some cases where there were obvious delays.

The case of the police record was especially dramatic. Another teacher who had already applied for her record explained the process to me. Since I was going in to Kingston, I offered her a ride. Because it was a long journey, I decided to change the two front wheels on the car since they had come with the car and needed to be changed. The tires were switched around with the back on the front and the new ones on the back. The next day we were on our way.

Emperor was doing well. Juliet and I chatted as we journeyed along the Bustamante highway. The sun was searing, but the little air condition unit in the Swift was putting up a brave fight. As we approached the roundabout near the Rio Mino Bridge, I heard a strange sound. After I bought Emperor, I soon learned to listen and respond to every sound I heard. So when I heard an odd whirr, I pulled to the side of the road and stopped.

When I got out, the back right wheel was still hissing as the air seeped out. I reasoned that I could pump some air in it, then drive to the nearest repair shop. Juliet and I took turns pumping, but it was to no avail. Upon closer examination, I realized that the valve had a cut where it met the tire —the new tire! So now our mission had changed. Thankfully, we were both wearing pants so it was time to change the wheel.

We got stones to block the wheels, removed the spare and jack from the trunk and started to work. I don't think those guys who had put on the wheel intended for them to come off again. We didn't just work —we struggled and labored, but without success. Sweat was trickling down my back and wherever else it had a mind to.

I was running out of ideas when a fast car pulled up. Two young men jumped out. I whispered a quick prayer to Jehovah. This is Jamaica; you don't play with your life. There were enough stories of gunmen hijacking cars along the road. We were good game—sitting ducks, as they say.

"Hello, Miss, you need some help?" One of them was bounding toward us and the other was right behind him. I wasn't about to look the gift horse in its mouth.

"Oh yes, we certainly do. The valve is broken and I can't get the tire off."

"Hey, Marky, checkout the situation and see what we need."

This was the other young man, who was the driver of the sports car. He was coming toward us and issuing instructions as he walked. You would have thought that we had merely made a pit stop.

"So you have problems getting it off," he said, bending down to take a look. "This jack not good man. Hey, Marky—carry the jack and the lug tool!" He was assertive and sure of himself. I liked that.

"Can you believe that I just changed the tires yesterday?" I asked trying to be helpful.

"They never change the valve dem." This was his expert reply. He spoke well and was clean cut which was indicative. He would not have been an ordinary gunman, I thought, and I started to relax.

"I'm Marjorie and this is my friend, Juliet. I now know that he is Marky," I said nodding toward the other young man getting the tools from the back of his car. "That leaves you." I was trying to lighten the situation. My policy has always been first attack is best defense. Usually this attack came in the form of conversation. I reasoned that if the person is talking with me he may not be so quick to do me harm.

"Oh, I'm Daniel. Where is your key?" I knew he meant the special part to put over the lug nut. This was not the first time that I had to have tires changed and, thankfully, I have always had help or have to hand the person this tool.

By this time Marky was back. I think they changed that tire in less than three minutes. We discovered that they raced cars and did their own repairs. That explained why they were so efficient at changing tires. We were back in business. They were back in their car and were gone. It was as though they were never there. I thanked them profusely before they left.

"Juliet, you know what I learned from this experience?"

"That the Lord is good and he provides for us in his own time?"

"That too, but I was thinking of another aspect of his goodness. You realized how long we were trying to pull that tire? I usually think I am so strong, but those men made it seem as if I wasn't even trying. So when the Bible says, 'Woman is the weaker vessel', you see what it means? We all have our roles in this life."

"That is so true," she agreed and we were both quiet for awhile as we reflected on the idea.

We got to New Kingston just in time. I paid for the Police Record, and then traveled to Duke Street, downtown Kingston to submit it there. Juliet was collecting hers, but I had to sit and sit and wait and wait before I completed the process. I had no idea that so many people applied for this document each day. It makes me wonder what the government does with all that money.

Since I had to leave, I asked whether I could have my cousin stop by and pick up the completed record and they said yes.

Ann, my cousin, worked near the area. When she went, the document was not ready. She called me and allowed me to speak to one of the officers on duty. He wanted to know who to send the record to. All this information is on the form. I patiently explained it again. About half-an-hour later, they called back with the same question. I explained again. I know that he was just playing for time. The next call was to say there was no one to type it. This is the same record for which I had paid an expedition fee, they were really hoping for a "greasing of the palm." In the end it was my cousin who had to sit and type it. Finally, I had the record. Thankfully, the transcripts were to be sent directly to the agency.

I sent off all the documents I had gathered and the other email came.

> *"Thank you for your interest in our program. We value your diligence and commitment… We look forward to having you on board!"*

Sacrifice would have been a better choice of word, but "diligence and commitment" could work. I could live with that.

Every step of the way, I brought Liz up-to-date. She dutifully marveled at the work involved and remarked, "But, Marj, it is like another degree you doing! Boy, you good! Well, I jus' hope an' pray that in the end it is worth it."

"I only hope so too. I'm at step four now."

"So what happens at step four?"

"We have to gather any outstanding documents and prepare a five minutes lesson to teach at the personal interview when we go to Kingston."

"You mean you have another interview and you have to teach too!" She was incredulous. "Boy, Marj, it's too much! Me tell you the truth, you really good!"

"Aright man, a hear you. But sometimes you do what you have to do. The work itself not hard you know, it's just inconvenient because of the other things that I have to do and the fact that I don't have the internet at home."

"They should consider that you guys are still teaching and all that work... no sir, not me."

"I suppose this could be a part of the test. This is more than multi-tasking. If we complete the process successfully, we should be able to handle the workload in the States."

"I suppose." She obviously was not convinced "So when is this teaching and interview?"

"It's April 6th at the Pegasus."

"2007 starts off hectic e man? Then la-la! The 6th is not a holiday? You sure it's the 6th?"

"The 6th is a holiday? Which holiday?"

"It's Good Friday."

"Well, I better find out if they know that it's a holiday here. As you know, when it comes to these religious holidays I'm thoroughly confused, I'm really clueless."

There was no mistake; they knew it was a holiday. They had chosen it so as not to conflict with the normal school schedule. How thoughtful! Since I had gathered the required documents and had sent them off via courier, I needed to plan my five minutes lesson and focus on the interview. Practice makes improvement and I had had a lot of practice. Being a Witness and attending the Theocratic Ministry School and Service meetings at the Kingdom Hall each week provides me with many opportunities.

Every Witness knows how to make an effective presentation in five minutes. We learn to make interest arousing introductions, display enthusiasm and warmth, ask view point questions, demonstrate poise, use repetition for emphasis, logically develop material, and use effective illustrations, visual aids, sound arguments and effective conclusion. So if I am not overcome by nerves, then I should be able to do the same for the lesson. I set about planning my five-minute lesson. I provided information for the hypothetical case. It would be a group of grade eleven students and this would be five minutes of a seventy-minute lesson. There would be about forty students and the general topic is Comprehension, but we would be focusing on Poetry and how symbols are used to convey different levels of meaning.

RATIONALE

Paper Two of the external examination tests understanding and expression skills. Understanding skills operate at two levels. At the first level you can understand the literal meaning or factual information. At the second level you can understand other aspects of meaning based on the use of symbols and images.

Poetry provides the stiffest challenges to students. Regrettably, in their report, the examiners say that candidates do not respond satisfactorily. A poem is often much more than an intellectual exercise. A poem expresses feelings as well. Students need to spend time developing their ability to analyze poems.

SKILLS TO BE DEVELOPED
Students should be able to:

- understand the different meanings and levels of meaning
- understand the techniques which the poet/ writer uses to convey this meaning
- express what they think, clearly and briefly

SPECIFIC OBJECTIVES:
At the end of the lesson, students should be able to:

- identify the basic elements used in a given poem. (Symbols, images)
- explain how the images are created
- express in their own words the literal meaning of the poem
- explore the idea of other level of meaning for the same symbols

STUDENTS' ACTIVITIES
Students will:

- dramatize, observe a skit, discuss and respond to the teacher,
- read the poem
- identify the facts in the poem and the devices used
- explain the meaning of the poem being discussed

PROCEDURE
INTRODUCTION
A Skit. A boy will offer a girl a rose. The girl puts up her palm and tells him to talk to the hand.

The students will relate what they deduced from the drama. How do the boy and girl feel about each other? What creates that impression?

They should conclude that the boy likes the girl, but the feeling is not mutual. This is conveyed by the rose offered which is a symbol of love. The girl's distaste, objection and rejection of the boy are shown in the upraised hand, which suggests; keep away from me.

The teacher writes the word, symbol, on the board and students are reminded of the meaning. (A symbol is a thing that represents something else.) The teacher explains that symbols are used to convey meaning in our lives and writers often use symbols in an effective way to convey meaning.

DEVELOPMENT

The papers with the poem are given to students. The students will read the poem. They will express what they understand from the poem. The teacher will question them to elicit the first level of meaning.

The facts of the poem will be written on the board:

- the wall with slogans
- the old black woman
- the ruins
- the cars and the traffic lights

Students will be helped to arrive at the first level of meaning. The woman could symbolize the very poor, scavenging while the cars (symbolizing the well-to-do) are idle (the idle rich?).

STUDENTS' WORK

The poet is not merely describing a simple scene, but is drawing from us a response to a situation that goes beyond the individual woman. Since the poem is entitled "Jamaica 1979," a whole further range of meanings become possible. Imagine that the woman is Jamaica.

- Find out what was happening in Jamaica in 1979.
- Do some research on the political and social conditions that prevailed at that time
- Use a map to locate Jamaica and identify where Cuba and the United States are in relation to it. Say how these countries could be represented in the poem.

RESOURCES

- Students to perform
- A rose
- Excerpt from text <u>CXC English A Study Guide</u>, Poem 'Jamaica 1979' by Mervyn Morris,
- Chart with illustration of the poem

EVALUATION

Homework- Do research (Details to be provided)

It was prudent to stay in or near the location for the appointment. I called Lav, my friend in Spanish Town, and arranged accommodations. I made sure that Emperor was up for the trip and set about packing. I had to ensure that my teaching aids, handout and other related materials were in my case. I ironed my clothes and cleaned my shoes just so I would not have anything to do, but the essential. The idea was to be relaxed and unhurried. Emperor and I set out for Angel Estate early enough so that we would be there before dark and so that Lav and I could play catch-up-and-fill-in before I went to bed.

Next day, Good Friday, traffic was easy like Sunday morning and Emperor cruised into the Pegasus parking lot with time to spare. Mentally, I was ticking off the dos-and-don'ts for interviews. Arrive on time and locate the area for the meeting. Use the rest room before presenting myself. While I was washing my hands in the rest room, I saw a young woman. She was tall, white and athletic in appearance. Her pale blue eyes lit up above her rosy cheeks as she smiled in response to my greeting. We made some idle comment--about what I can't even remember. Sometimes the subject is non-essential; it's just the warmth of the smile or gesture of kindness one stranger to another that forges that continued link of humanity. We went our separate ways and my mind went back to the task at hand.

When I arrived at the room named in the letter, there were four people. It struck me as odd that there were no signs of readiness for such an event as that for which we were gathering. The room was empty except for four chairs set out haphazardly across the floor. We chatted nervously, each trying to not let it show.

I introduced myself. "Good morning everybody, my name is Marjorie." There was a chorus reply, then an attempt to get in the names. I recognized one face. This was a great feat because her face was so discolored I was trying desperately not to stare. If I had seen her on the street or Down Town I would have mistaken her for one of the average bleachers. In college her face was very clean and smooth. She was visibly shaky; I tried to get her to relax.

"You did live over Big Yard, no true?" Big Yard is the name we gave to the largest cluster of dormitory on the Church Teachers College campus.

"Yes, I use to live on Swaby. You went to CTC?" I know she wouldn't remember me. She was in her final year and I was in my first. Moreover, as my friend Lucinda will tell you, you may not see me if I don't want you to see me. She had experienced it firsthand. I have learned to stand out or to blend in, depending on the crowd.

"Yes, I see you don't remember me—but don't feel bad, I've gotten use to that. It's as they say—it's not who you know; it's—"

"—who know you!" She finished the adage and made a weak attempt to laugh.

I thought she could do without the attention so I turned to another Churchite. Ludford and I were in the same year group. He did Mathematics and Science, I think, and I had done English and PE. We sometimes met in the gym and played volleyball. And his life had been colorful to date. He had endured family tragedy, completed his degree, taught at UWI and like me was itching for a change. We tried to play catch-up, asking after friends we had not seen or had last seen. I soon became aware that we were being selfish.

"Ludford, we better talk about something the others can share in. So, anybody know what to expect today?"

"I hear that we have to do a test," somebody supplied. Now that was news to me and to Shauna, the woman from college.

"Laud Jesus, a lie!" was all she could get out.

I was beginning to think that maybe it was not such a good idea to take that line. Some people don't handle stress very well and this was proving to be stressful for some people. Others were arriving and it was clear that the chairs were inadequate. Time was moving along and yet there was no sign of anyone who seemed official enough to be conducting the interviews. Soon someone came to inform us that it was not the room to be used. There were some miscommunications and so we all trooped downstairs to the new location.

The first person I saw when I entered the room was the lady from the ladies room. At that point there were about twelve people present. The lady, whom I will call Julia, was with a man, whom I will call Mark. They were to conduct the interviews and handle the day's proceedings. The group was divided in two, some moved to the adjoining room and the others would remain where we were meeting. I chose to stay and so did Julia. By this time I was being shadowed by Shauna. She sat next to me at the table.

Julia gave us the timetable for the day. We would introduce ourselves, do the teaching exercise, complete the written test and then sit for the personal interview. While I understood that it was a bit much, I could appreciate the significance. Since people can be so dishonest, anybody could have written the essay and lesson plan previously submitted, but it should be a bit of a challenge to beat this part of the process. Although my teeth and knees were knocking, I thought, "Bring it on!" I just had a good feeling about the whole thing, perhaps it was because I was well rested. I also knew I had to be strong because Shauna was beginning to lean on me. As soon as I tried to zone out and to focus on what was ahead, she had another question.

"You tink de test a go hard?"

"You did know say we did a go do dis too?"

"What you tink dem a go ask in de interview?"

"You can help me wid de test?"

"You fi ask me some question and practice wid me fi de interview—you hear?"

I knew I had to intervene in order to maintain my sanity and to give both of us a good shot at this thing.

"My girl—just cool no man! You making both of us nervous now. Try to think about something else. Me sure say you just working up yourself over nothing."

"A true—a true, a'right den, me a go read over me lesson."

"Good idea!" Oh sweet relief, now we could both focus.

With that, we both lapsed into what I hope was deep concentration. From the introduction, I realized that I was in the minority. There was a concentration of mathematics teachers—Michael, Petagay, Pearline and Ludford were teachers of Math, Shauna was Science and I was English. The presentation took place in almost the same order. We were to be the students and Julia was in place to evaluate.

First, up was Michael—talk about quietly achieving important goals? That was Michael. Now, I am going to tell you something in the strictest air of confidentiality: I don't like Math, never did. But when Michael got up there and started to do his thing in that calm, controlled and creative way, I began to think that maybe I had not given Math a chance.

Petagay was just as the latter part of her name suggests. She was enthusiastic and bounded around the room with her cake and pizza slices cut out of life-sized pictures. She was teaching fraction to a younger group of students. She was equally appealing and was very engaging.

After they had presented, it was time for the star pupil, Pearline. She played the part of student very well; the others of us had started to call her teacher's pet. While she was a good student, play acting and giving support by providing correct responses, she ran into problems in her own presentation. I think what happened was this; she had planned to teach one topic, but when she saw how well the others were doing teaching fractions, she decided to teach fractions too. The lesson was not related to the work sheets and home work she had planned to use. Even though I am no good at Math, I could have seen the problem. The result was fragmented and confusing.

Shauna also got into trouble with her presentation. She was shaking and her voice was quivering. I had gone up with her because she wanted me to demonstrate the use of force and energy. I was asked to erase the writing from the board. She then used a broom to sweep and then she asked the class to say what was happening. She kept sweeping harder and asking the same question when the students were not responding.

I think she started off well before it went downhill. Soon it was not clear what was being taught. The questions were sometimes ambiguous as she did not provide enough contexts to guide the students' responses. As the presentation fell apart, so did her confidence. When she was told the time was up she was still going around the room. And when she sat, she was first to remark that it did not go according to plan. That got me off the hook. It's one thing to know that you performed below standard, but, especially because I had not presented and I did not know how it would end, I did not want to be providing any negative feedback at that stage. I encouraged her to let that go and to focus on the rest of the day's activities. Moreover, there were still other presentations to be made, including mine and I thought it was best to concentrate on what was yet to come.

Ludford was up next and he did not disappoint. He used an interesting setting. He started out by returning graded papers of students' responses from the previous class. The lesson was based on some observations he had made when he was grading the work. Apparently, some students did not reflect mastery of the concept taught and so he was teaching it again. I thought that was smart as it would give him a lot of basis to refer to what was said in the last class.

He made reference to some of the mathematics masters. I actually sat up and started to pay attention when he started to discuss Pythagoras and his influence on Plato and Socrates. Ludford was adroit in his explanation of the principle of the

Pythagoras Theorem, I was most impressed. I just love that kind of teaching where you get good bargain for your attention and your willingness to learn. I think he did what an excellent teacher should do to students—he made me think. This was fascinating to me because it is the stuff that good arguments are made of in English or language arts. You must have assertions, logics, and proofs and be able to manipulate symbols. While I could never work out those problems he had assigned the students (I am convinced that I am dyslexic when it comes to math), I was able to follow the logic of his reasoning. When he was finished, I had no doubt that he was on his way to the USA.

Then it was my turn. I could not hide anymore; the fat lady was waiting in the wings for her cue. I needed assistance. So before the class, I had asked Ludford and Petagay if they were willing to do the demonstration. They agreed and I left them outside the room.

After greeting the class, I did a quick review.

"As I stood by the door, I heard your math teacher discussing Pythagoras Theorems. I'm sure nobody in this class knew that there is a relationship between Math and English." They laughed and said to the effect that there was no relationship.

"Your teacher of math explained the importance of understanding symbols if you're to master the subject and the same is true for Language and especially Poetry. Now, I know that many of you are not particularly fond of poetry, but I promise you that, after today, you'll see things differently and if you still don't like it—well…"

I had given Ludford a single long stem red rose. He was to present it to the girl and she would hold up her hand and refuse it. I had written the topics on the board and the words: Symbol and Meaning.

"Please take careful notice of the title on the board—as you observe this demonstration, what do you think you should be looking for?"

"Symbols and meanings!" they chorused.

"Very good. Excuse me while I get the door." I opened the door and Petagay and Ludford walked into the room – all was quiet. They walked to the front of the class in silence.

> He: Petagay, please accept this and believe me when I say I am very sorry. *[He offers her the rose and his voice cracks a little with nerves and emotion—very emotive]*
>
> She: Ludford, *[Breathes deeply, rolls eyes, hand akimbo, pouts]* You know what? Just talk to the hand. *[She holds up her hand palm facing him and fingers pointing in the air, flounces and turns her back—freezes.]*

The class broke out in applause. I could not have gotten a better performance if I had written and rehearsed it with them. They were good.

"Thank you very much, Petagay and Ludford. Okay, let's continue. Somebody, please tell me what just happened."

They started to respond together in a chorus.

"Just a minute now, I know after that duet performed so well, you want to hear a choir, but what if we take the soloists first." They laughed, and then quieted down before raising their hands. "Thank you." I took their responses one at a time.

"The boy is in love with the girl, but the girl doesn't like him."

"How can you tell?"

"He's giving her a red rose, but she gives him the hand."

"Why does he give her a rose and not, let's say—a fruit?"

"Because red rose symbolize love."

I jotted down red rose under symbol and love under meaning.

"Was there any other symbol?"

"Yes, Miss, the girl's hand."

"What did that say?"

"Stop, stay away, I don't want to talk to you."

"Based on what we have learned so far, what would you say is a symbol?"

"Something that means something else, Miss."

I corroborated their responses and wrote the meanings on the board. All this took place in about two-and-a-half minutes.

"Now for the poem. Symbols are very important in language. They are especially needed in creating vivid images in poems. Here is a poem of seven lines, but it is packed with meaning. Please follow on your sheets as I read, and pay attention to the symbols used. Let's see how they contribute to the meaning." I read the poem, then asked them to read it.

"Please tell me, what did you see in this poem?"

"Wall with revolutionary slogans"

"An old woman."

"Stones"

"Traffic light."

"Car."

I had drawn the picture described in the poem by juxtaposing the images. I displayed the picture and they agreed that it reflected what they had imagined. Like students of Science, we dissected that poem. I was not play acting. I was teaching because I could sense that they were genuinely interested in the different levels of meanings. I always love this part of teaching a lesson, when I feel as if I have them floating on a thought. Everything I say is like a puff of wind or a wave that propels them farther into freedom. They are hanging on every word, surfing on ideas and floating. As they are transported into the world of poetry, nothing else matters.

After we had established the first level of meaning, I drew their attention to yet another level of meaning and teased them a little. Confident that their desire to know more was fully aroused, I directed their attention to the homework. Always the best place to stop. Leave them wanting more and tell them how to satisfy what you hope is a growing appetite that can only be gratified by researching, meditating and stimulating discussions.

Julia was smiling and, based on the comments from the others, I had every reason to feel good. I had done my best and I was pleased. We did the test after the presentations. The tests were specific to the subject, so there was not much we could do to help each other. My test consisted of about five short answer questions and we all had to do an essay as well. The questions were testing for our knowledge of the content area, methodology and procedure. The essay was focused more on behavior management and evaluation.

We were encouraged to go for lunch after we had completed our test and to return in time for our appointment. Since I was scheduled for four-thirty in the afternoon, I gladly accepted the urgings of the others to go into New Kingston for lunch. That was not to be. Shauna begged me to stay with her. I stayed. She wrote. I proofread. She did her interview, called her husband and left. Just like that, she was gone.

While we were in the lobby I met Megan, who was in the other room. She is a teacher of Spanish. We chatted until it was time for her to go in. By this time I was hungry. Because it was so late I decided to try the hotel restaurant. The only thing I could afford on the menu was a sandwich. It is the most expensive sandwich I have eaten to this day. I still think of it as my, Sandwich a la Shauna.

Julia and I were the only two left. We were both weary from the long day. It was at this point that my nerves gave way. Whatever Shauna had in the morning, I now had it! My feet refused to stay on the ground. I tried locking my knees, but they were knocking as if they were hearing some up tempo beat. We, Julia and I, smiled at each other. Hers reassuring; mine was Whoopi Goldberg-like, more cheeks and lips than eyes and teeth.

"You won't believe how nervous I am!" that just came out.

"But why? You performed so well this morning! You were so confident."

"I don't know. My knees are just knocking." We both laughed. Hardly the start I wanted, but this is one of my weaknesses. At least some of my friends think so. I can be a little too open at times, but it works for me. Why hide when I know that you know that I am trembling? Let's remove the secrecy. If my body wants to tremble, let it. I was ready for that interview. We tried to put on our professional airs and she encouraged me. "What did you think of your presentation this morning?"

"I thought it went well. Were you able to follow the lesson?"

"Yes. I was able to follow easily. You seemed quite comfortable."

"Thank you. Did you understand the different levels of meaning and the symbols used?'

"Yes. It was an interesting choice of poem. I think I will read it again."

"That was my objective, so I would say I met my objective. I like the way the lesson flowed. I think Petagay and Ludford did very well in introducing the topic. It was one way of getting the children involved." I asked her about her teaching experience. We spoke about that briefly. I decided that I was chatting too much because of my nerves.

Julia had another question. "It was very good the way you connected the other subject area as well. Tell me, how would you have adjusted this lesson so that you could cater to the students with limited abilities?"

"Of course we are operating under the assumption that this is not my first lesson with these students, so I should have knowledge of their limitations. There are a number of things that I could have done, especially if they were having difficulty understanding. I could have allowed them to illustrate the poem themselves. I could have allowed them to work in pairs so that they can share ideas. Or I could have used music. There are many songs that speak about inequality in the society as well as the response of the oppressed. We could use clippings from the newspaper or pictures from Up Town and Down Town Kingston or Jamaica and a Metropolitan country, among other things."

She was writing as I spoke and sometimes I tried to hold back the ideas that were rearing to cut-and-run. She smiled and was ready once again.

"You know that if you are selected to teach in the U.S., you will be sharing your culture. How could you have used this lesson to impart or share aspects of your culture?"

"The truth is English lends itself to cultural exchange quite easily. Language is an expression of its user, the people and how they live. You may recall that in the introduction of the lesson, I actually had Petagay perform an act which is part of the North American culture: 'Talk to the hand!' In the Jamaican culture, the children may say, 'Chat to me back, but no chat to me front!' This would be followed by the same body language. Basically, they are both saying the same thing and the victims would feel the same way." My jaws were beginning to ache. If you think it was easy try smiling, talking and preventing your teeth from chattering all at the same time.

"That's really interesting. It's good to see that you had a good interaction with your students and this seemed natural. We both know that children can be a challenge at times. How do you manage students' behavior?"

"I must confess that real disruptive behavior has been more the exception than the norm for me over the years. For the few occasions though when they do occur, there are some written procedures for particular conduct. Our school has a Disciplinary Policy that both students and parents sign. As teachers we review it with the students. Therefore, we are aware of the conduct and the consequence. Some behaviors are zero tolerance and the teacher is at liberty to apply her discretion in some other cases. We may take some measures in the classroom to discourage negative conduct. We have teacher, office then parents. Parents are called in as a last resort.

I try to teach my students the power of communal responsibility. They have to understand that all are affected badly when they misbehave or are disruptive. So I hope to influence them with positive peer pressure.

What I find though is this, they are willing to take part in the planned activities and the majority of them express a willingness to learn so I try to do my part to ensure that the lessons will engage them. If you like I could relate a recent example."

"Yes, yes, please go ahead."

"Last week I went to a class. When I got there the teacher had already left. As I entered the room a girl asked to go to the restroom. The rule is to ask the last teacher for permission so that you may go during the transition. When I asked her why she hadn't asked earlier, she became upset.

"I started to greet the class and she began to shout at me. I asked her to wait for me by the door and she hissed and stormed out. Some girls near the door began to laugh.

"She returned to class about ten minutes later and went to her seat. I asked her once again to wait for me by the door, but she started to quarrel loudly and the class was cheering her on. The Form Teacher was passing and entered the room to see what was happening. The student refused to yield even then.

"I reported the matter myself. When the VP called us to his office, she had the student council rep speak for her. She was most apologetic and was asking that the incident not go on her record because she wanted to run for a position on the Student Council.

We told her she should have considered the consequence of her action and the implication for her future.

"I was lenient with her, although some may not think I was. I had her sweep the grass that was on the quadrangle from the mowing in the morning and asked her to apologize in class. I reprimanded the rest of the class for their tacit support; although they knew what she was doing was wrong. She has been a model student since that day."

"Wow!" Julia said. We chatted a little about the forms of behavior that pose a challenge to the teaching learning process before moving on to the other question. Julia remarked, "You seem to enjoy teaching."

"I do. I really do. When you think of it, I am always teaching, spiritually or secularly, and I love it."

"What are some methods of evaluation you use in your classroom?"

"Over the years, I have found it essential to vary the teaching methods and the mode of assessing or evaluating learning. The school has SWAT or Six Week Assessment Tests and the end of term exams. However, outside of that, thankfully, we are at liberty to vary our methods. I have found that it is encouraging to use different methods to cater to the learning styles and varied abilities. I used tests, portfolio or scrapbooks assessments, group projects, oral presentations among other things."

Again I paused to allow her to complete her notes and to catch my own breath. She wanted to know what plans I was making in order to make the move.

I explained that I would sell my car rent two flats at my house and make arrangements for someone to oversee things. The house could pay for its own maintenance, so I was not worried about it. It would also service my insurance and care for my mother.

"That's good to know that you have your own house. You seem so young, yet obviously you have thought this through. Do you think you will find it hard to be away from your home?"

"No. For me my home was one dream to fulfill, but not an end. Now that I have accomplished that, I want to go after some other dreams, like teaching abroad for the next three years and completing my Masters Degree."

"That's very good. I like the way you have thought out and set your objectives. What do you believe is going to be your greatest challenge teaching abroad?" She had her pen poised to write. I really gave this one some thought. Yet the answer was clear.

"The students!" I startled myself.

"The students?" She asked, sounding surprised. "Why the students?"

"I am thinking that adults would have learned the art of hypocrisy. They are more sophisticated, for want of a better expression. But children are usually less concerned about being subtle in their feelings toward others. They want to do things to please and amuse their peers, while the adults may be somewhat inhibited by their good manners or something."

We both laughed at this thought, but agreed that children can be a challenge to contend with. Then it was my turn to ask questions. I had read a lot of the material that the agency had posted online. In addition, I had asked my Teacher Advisor most of the other relevant questions. Since they were not the people to provide the job, there was not a lot that I could ask her. There was one thing I wanted to know. "My knowledge of schools in the U.S. comes mainly from the media. I have students from the States from time-to-time, but never ones I'd be proud to write home about. How reflective of the realities in the American schools are the movies such as *"Lean on Me"*, *"Dangerous Minds"* and some of those comedies we see on TV, with the classroom setting?"

While they were extreme cases, those events did occur in some schools. Julia was not from the U.S., but from Canada. So I asked about the "No Broken Glass Policy." I think I would like to visit that region sometime.

"That reminds me, have you read *Ann of Green Gables?*"

It was not long before we were mentally touring the Prince Edward Islands and recapping the details of other stories in the series. Alice Montgomery would have felt proud that she could unite two strangers through her work.

We could have gone on and on, but, alas, life is not like that. Julia was planning to go walking in Emancipation Park, something she had gotten in the habit of doing at the end of the work day in order to unwind. I know what walking in that park is like. I walked there late at night when the sun is out of the sky. It is a whole new world, like miles away from the chaos and mayhem of Maxfield Avenue. I had a two-hour drive ahead of me, back to St. Elizabeth, so we got moving. The interview had finished except for the video segment. All the nerves that had fled suddenly returned with a vengeance. All I remember from that segment was the end when Julie laughed and said, "Oh, there it is. I was wondering what had happened to that warm, beautiful smile."

Apparently I was so tense I was not even smiling which is rare. We were glad to have met each other, but glad the interrogation had ended. We said our goodbyes, but hoped we would meet again.

All this took place after I got back from Antigua. I had gone there to participate in a wedding. It was during the Cricket World Cup period and the schools in some islands were out for the event. The wedding was planned with this in mind, but it did not work out very well for me. Since I had given my word to attend I had to stay by it. The schools in Jamaica were not all granted time off, only those in the immediate vicinity of the Sabina Park, one of the stadiums where the game was being played. It meant that I had to apply for the time off from school. I went and was part of the wedding drama--and drama it was—but when I got back I paid dearly. Apparently I was not advised correctly about my application for leave. So the Ministry instructed the Bursar or, as we liked to call him, the Exchequer, to deduct salary for the days taken, which included the weekend. Based on the first deduction and the projection, I would be repaying more than I was earning, for each day, over a six-month period. There was a great outcry about the injustice. It was one more push for me to go. How much of this could I take?

They say when it rains it pours and the Jamaican expression which is even more suitable is: Trouble no set like rain. If it did, I would have saved a whole lot of money that week. My friends, Carey and Kelly, agreed to accompany me to the airport. The plan was that I would drive Emperor and they would take it back, keep it and then come back for me at the airport. Because I was not due to leave until the afternoon, I went in to school the morning to avoid taking that extra day. There were some other events that contributed to some further delay, but we were off in good time. I was driving. I decided to use both toll roads to save time and we were doing very well.

I was urging Emperor on to the finish. We were chatting merrily as we—I will not say sped—but went along. When I heard the sound, at first I thought it was merely my imagination. I asked the others whether they had heard it too, but they hadn't. I slowed and it seemed to stop. It sounded like the rasping you hear when someone is having difficulty breathing. Only, there was the metallic chortle that suggested that more was going on. It was not until we were within sight of the airport that I saw the steam coming from the bonnet. The gauge was way past hot. I pulled over to the side of the road and opened the hood. At first glance, everything was red. I was forced to step back from the heat that was issuing from it.

We stood there asking each other what was the best course. The time was not on our side.

"You think I could get a ride from here?" I wondered aloud.

"Dem not going stop here so Sis." That was Kelly's take on the matter. In truth, I would be afraid to just hop a ride in Kingston. I laughed. What else could I do? I was so near and yet so far. We all hissed our teeth in despair. That is the Jamaican solution to most problems. Somehow the act seemed to either cause the matter to dissipate or clear the fog from the brain thus allowing you to see the issue clearer.

"I tell you what; I know it had enough of everything for the journey. I had the oil and coolant checked. Something else is wrong. I will drive it up to the airport and you see if you can get someone on the way to fix it so that you can drive home."

We did just that. We said some quick goodbyes and I gave a little money to help and I was gone. I ran all the way. There was no one in line, but me. It was a mad rush all the way. I was very careful about spending in Antigua because I knew I had to pay for whatever it cost to get that car back on the road.

When I returned, Emperor was still not fixed. It had been taken to the mechanic and the engine had been taken out. I had the name of a man who deals in Swift parts so we went there from the airport. I was able to take home a used engine. Yes, it was more money, but it was necessary spending. In addition, I was also aware that I was still in the preparation process to resettle overseas for a short period.

When I got back I received this invitation.

Jamaica Placement Fair
March 29, 2007

We would like to inform you of a Placement Fair in Montego Bay on Saturday May 19. Several U.S. school districts will attend the Placement Fair in order to interview teachers and offer positions for the upcoming school year. Attending a Placement Fair provides you with a wonderful chance to secure a teaching position. If you are successful at your personal interview and have a complete application / documents package, we will send you an invitation to attend the Placement Fair. Only teachers who are invited ...are able to attend. Registration is required.

We are looking forward to meeting you soon.

The wait would not be too long. I really wanted to speed things up so I could be sure how to arrange my activities, time and money. So I was pleased when I received this.

Successful Personal Interview
April 12, 2007

Congratulations on completing your____ personal interview. You are one step closer to the adventure of a lifetime: teaching in the U.S.A. The next step in the admission process is to evaluate your eligibility for a U.S. teaching license...

You are now able to visit the ____ website where you can find __ an online pre-departure orientation. Please take time to complete the vital information about participation in the Program. You are responsible for reviewing this information and completing the learning courses prior to accepting a teaching position...

Completing those courses was beyond me. I tried to get through as many as I could, but given the fact that I was attempting to do them either during my lunch break or on Saturday at a cost, it was not possible to finish them. Moreover, another letter arrived.

*Pre-Departure Orientation
April 16, 2007*

To help you prepare for your cultural—exchange experience in the United States, we would like to invite you to the Program's Pre-departure Orientation session on Sunday, May 20. The Session will be held at the Half Moon Resort in Montego Bay 1:00-5:00 p.m.

…we hope you will take advantage of this opportunity to learn more about living and working in the U.S. *

Some of the topics that will be covered at this session include:

- *Cultural differences in U.S.A. classroom management*
- *Effective teaching strategies*
- *Classroom management and discipline in U.S classrooms.*
- *Rules, procedures, and consequences*

*(Please note that attendance at this event is not a guarantee of employment)

Just imagine, after all that effort, after going here and going there, doing this and doing that, now they were starting to direct my attention to the fine print. Attendance was not a guarantee of my employment. From here on, I expected more of these cautions would be appearing. It was like signing up to do a thirty-mile marathon for a prize money, then being told, after twenty miles, that there is a chance you may not receive the prize when you complete the race--even if you win!

Recommended for Placement
May 01, 2007

Marjorie: Congratulations on being recommended for a U.S teaching position with the __Program. During the coming months, we will share your credentials with U.S. school districts and match your experiences and preferences to the needs of individual schools.

Although you will work with us throughout the admission process, U.S schools, not us, make formal employment offers to all our teachers. We will promote your experience and skills to U.S. schools that are hiring. You will be guaranteed a position only when a U.S school district has offered you a contract.

The vast majority of our applicants recommended for teaching positions do receive an employment offer and teach in the U.S. for up to three years. However, a small number of our applicants do not... Since the needs of U.S. schools do change throughout the year, we cannot guarantee you a position.

Our staff and U.S. schools are considering you for English – High School...

We know you are excited about your placement recommendation...

Soon, you can share your culture with students and staff in the U.S.

I was really looking forward to it. I had started to collect samples of students' work, newspaper clippings, stamps, postcards, music, short story books, tourist brochures and anything Jamaican that I could find that I thought would interest teenagers. Now that I was Mo' Bay bound, I needed to find some place to spend the night in the second city. A night at a hotel, although appealing, was out of my league at that time. My financial reservoir was experiencing a minor drought.

A few years before when I attended a convention at Jarret Park, in Mo' Bay, my friend Cato had arranged for us to stay with a fellow Witness. After all my other options had fallen through, it dawned on me that perhaps that sister would be willing to accommodate me for the night. There were certain advantages to staying in this area. It was not far from the Half Moon Hotel and keep in mind that the idea is to stay near the place for the meeting. I doubted that she would remember me, but that did not matter. The important thing was that we were both Witnesses. That is the beauty of the organization. Even if we were meeting for the first time, after the first five minutes, we were like old friends. It has always amazed my relatives who are not Witnesses, how when I meet fellow worshippers we get on like we have always known each other and it does feel that way.

When I called her, Dr. B was as gracious as ever. We used a few minutes to become reacquainted. I had not forgotten her name because I have a few friends who were seeing her professionally. It was easier for me to remember her because she was the hostess. At the time, there were about twelve of us staying at her house for the convention in 2002. The final night we had dinner by the swimming pool and we discussed many issues of concern as we ate by candle light. Some of us were becoming acquainted as we were quite a mix from different parts of the world; others of us had known each other for some time. We were thrown closer together because of the power outage during dinner. I hope that the others have treasured the memory as I have these many years.

Although Emperor was doing well with the new engine, I had noticed a little oil leak. I decided to have it stopped before going to the dear doctor's house or traveling so far from home. While we were at it, I had the radiator cleaned and the engine washed. When you find out the answer to this one, please let me know. Why does it always rain after you spend time and money to have the car washed? It rained like the days of Noah were coming back. By the time I had traversed those pothole infested streets and those roads turned to rivers, I could almost swear that Emperor had developed a cold. There was a sound issuing from that bonnet that was very much like an asthma attack. I was glad that I had come to the end of the road for that night.

The last time I was there was in 2002, the summer before university and there I was again 2007, the spring before going to the U.S. My observation skills had come to my aid once again. After all these years I was able to find the house in the dusk without any problems. The lights outside the house and on the gate glowed weakly in the aftermath of the rain. I called from my phone and she released the gate which was controlled by remote. The rain had stopped, but the air was still moist and the clouds lingered threateningly. When I entered the house we greeted each other warmly and enquired of each other about how our day was spent.

I had settled in and was preparing the Watchtower article for the next day while she graded papers. It was after ten when her phone rang. One of her Bible students was at the hospital with her child who was suffering a severe asthma attack. She was alone at the hospital and she needed some assistance. We got dressed quickly and were back on the road. She drove this time and we were in her sport utility vehicle, so we went through the high waters with ease. I know that the young woman was heartened by the sacrifice and I was happy to have been a part of it even in that little way. That act of kindness endeared the doctor to me even more.

The next day I was up early. Some people never learn. The first thing I did was to give the car a wash. After all, I was going to the Kingdom Hall and to the Half-Moon Hotel. May it not be said that mine was the dirty car! The good doctor had fed me well with roast breadfruit, ackee and salt fish. We talked as she cooked and she told me about her anthology for which she was having a book signing party. I told her about my plans to migrate temporarily and my plans to put on a formal get-together for the friends before I left. There was a whole lot of sharing and I hope to finish some of those topics we started some day.

The meeting was spiritually upbuilding. As is my habit, I moved around and introduced myself before the meeting began. I was very pleased to meet some friends who were on vacation from the States. We introduced ourselves each, thinking that the other belongs to the local congregation. We all laughed when we learned that we were both visiting for the first time. They were on vacation from the States and were staying at a hotel in the vicinity. I maintain that the world is just filled with friends just waiting to be met and once you have met, chances are you will meet again.

I had prepared my clothes and had them hanging in the car; therefore, there was no need to iron. After the meeting

I headed to Iron Shore, this is a vibrant shopping area on the outskirts of the chain of hotels and some affluent homes over the hill. The shops were conveniently positioned in the middle of both areas and along a major road way. The skirt I wore to the Kingdom Hall was switched for a pair of pants in the bathroom at one Burger King Restaurant. Driving alone far away from home and in a dress has never appealed to me. I always like to be ready for any eventualities. Comfort and a sense of security was my priority and this habit has served me well over the years. If you have ever traveled via public transport in Jamaica, you appreciate the importance of modest, comfortable clothing.

On one occasion I was on my way to Kingston by bus. I took a taxi from Santa Cruz to Mandeville. That taxi, a sedan Volvo contained five people in the back seat made for four and three in the front seat made for two. We flew low over the hill from Santa Cruz to Mandeville. The only consolation was that because the car was so packed, the passengers could not be tossed about when the car rounded the hair pin turns and S-bends on Spur Tree Hill.

When I landed in Mandeville, I paid my fare to the driver and took a couple minutes to allow my blood to start circulating and my organs to settle back in the places designed for them. As the feelings began to return to my extremities, I collected my thoughts and my bags and headed toward the Kingston Bus Park. Initially I did not realize that the group of men racing toward me—was really coming to get me.

"One me wa! A one me wa!" the first one shouted holding up the index finger to make his point.

"Empress, rope in—we a move now!" this was a cool, Rasta man, who swept his locks back and stuffed his Pan-African colored rag in his pocket as he extended his hand to me as if he was really about to escort an empress.

"Town! Town! Up a Town! Up a Town we a go!" this man was sweating profusely giving more credence to the curse put up on Adam, 'By the sweat of your brow you shall eat bread.'

"Yow! 'llow de lady—a me she a go wid!" This was another man. He was huge and commanding, but this was a different jungle. The laws of the jungle apply too, but the smaller creatures lived by their wit and the big ones by their might and sometimes they just fight.

My heart was in overdrive. I knew I had to be careful as pickpockets often used this as an opportunity to start their work while they get up-close-and-personal. It was not unusual for bus drivers, conductors and touts to hackle travelers and start fights which sometimes ended in death or severe injury. Many of them carry knives on their person and may have machetes or guns in their vehicles. I clutched my handbag and my traveling case closer to my body and tried to stand my ground. Before I realized what was happening, a man snatched my bag and was moving quickly toward the line of buses. I clung to my handbag and tried to make my way through the crowd to keep him in sight. Then I felt myself suddenly air borne. Before I could recover from the shock of my bag being snatched and react appropriately or inappropriately, someone had picked me up and was carrying me physically. I was deposited on a seat in one of the buses, I in one bus and my bag in another. That was humiliating. I was never one to dream of a man to sweep me off my feet yet, there I was…

"Don' move my girl, me wi' get back you bag, sista." Of course I had never met him in my life, but they will be related to anybody they want to be their passenger.

The other passengers were amused. I was confounded. Nobody expected that one, least of all me. I stayed put, my bag came and I went to Kingston. I know that people have been killed for less than that, so I simply sat there and watched as they attacked each new person on the scene like a school of piranha. I was just glad to be wearing pants and to this day I always wear pants when I travel. Although I am not confronted by aggressive men fighting for a fare, now that I drive, I still have the challenges of punctures, engine trouble; you just never know.

After I changed my skirt for the pair of pants, I went to the pharmacy and got some thank-you cards. I had already written a note to my hostess so these were for the panel that I would meet at the Placement Fair. I ate the snack I bought at Burger King and then set out for the hotel.

The whole place was like a little village. I felt as though I was in a maze as I drove around the buildings. After stopping for directions twice, I finally arrived at the building I sought. There were a few cars in the parking lot, but no one in sight. I parked quickly and headed to the main area for registration. That was where the early birds were gathered. Upon arrival, I immediately started to look around for those I had seen in Kingston and to become reacquainted. Teachers were still arriving and the air was abuzz with chatter. There was no sign of Shauna and Pearline, but I saw the others and even some from university and college days. Michael was there with his wife and I met some other spouses. The most pleasant surprise for me was meeting a former student.

She was there with a friend and her sister. Before we knew it, we were strolling down memory lane. I made enquiries about other students that I had not seen since they graduated.

We were given packages with the day's itinerary and then we went to the conference center where we met members of the team and some representatives from the different school districts. It was beginning to unfold. Ludford and I were sitting together with Michael and his wife near us. After the preliminaries we were advised to check our packages for a slip of paper. Those of us who had been short-listed would have pink slips with the name of the school district's rep who wished to meet with us. Ludford, Michael, Donna and I were to meet with Dr. Johns from Vance County in North Carolina. There were other representatives and we discussed the possibility of meeting with them as well.

The dinner was a good introduction into the cultural differences. The presentation was a picture. There was a lot of food and the variety was breath taking-- literally at some points, such as the section with the cheeses, where I could not endure the odor. The roast beef had most of us gagging as the life was still oozing in some places. I was pleased to see that I was not the only one for whom the rare meat had no appeal. Thankfully, because of the variety of the menu, we were able to get other foods to satisfy our appetites. More than the food though, I think it was stimulating to be among so many people who had just gone through a similar experience and were about to embark on yet another.

It was a long line for the interview appointments. Even those of us who were short-listed had a long wait. Based on what I had noticed on the brochure, Vance County did not need many teachers for the secondary level, which was my preference. I realized that they would not be able to place all of the teachers of English. Donna and I explored the possibility of not being placed, but we were hopeful. We were most impressed by the presentation of the rep from that county and were anticipating the interview.

"You know it would be nice if all o' we go to the same place." Ludford was already grinning from ear to ear at the thought.

"That would be good. They seem to need more Math than English teachers though. We have to consider the possibility that we may not all end up at the same place." I was trying to be realistic.

Some teachers were getting signed right away. There were only about four school districts represented, so we knew not all of us would have been placed at the fair. Late in the afternoon, we began getting called in. The Math people were signed right away, but I saw only one teacher of English for the middle-school level who had been placed. Donna had gone in before me and I was really looking forward to my time. When Donna came out, we didn't have time to talk because it was my turn to face the music. I went to the room and did the textbook stuff. I greeted the interviewer and introduced myself; she invited me to take a seat. We got through the usual questions and I commended her on her presentation which I found to be very informative. I think she was friendly and warm. I liked her. She had an easy way about her. She laughed genuinely and made me feel relaxed.

"Miss Wright, one of the main reasons we are trying to get some outstanding teachers, is because we desire to provide these kids with some positive role models. Many of them are from depressed areas and they have no real successful examples in their immediate experience, especially among people of color."

She sounded genuine enough and went on to express a desire for especially families to move in the area and to be visible. That helped to explain it. The other teacher who was already signed had her family with her. I could see her in the background feeding the baby as she spoke. She talked about the salary and the bonus that was offered by the district. We talked and I thought that I could do well in that area. There would be enough money for me to take care of my needs. I just wanted to make sure that I was not earning less than I did in Jamaica and that I would not live below the standard I had enjoyed at home. We tied up the interview and she gave me some information including her email address, encouraged me to keep in touch and promised that by the Wednesday I should hear from her school district.

By the time we got out it was time to move on to the other area where the orientation fair would be held. The rain was getting ready again for what appeared to be a night on the town, but I was not too concerned because I would be inside a building cool and dry for the next few hours. The wet roads I would deal with when the session was finished. They never stopped telling us how special we were to be selected from so many hundreds of applicants. The presenters proceeded to establish their own credentials that made them qualified to share with us what would work in the U.S. classroom and what would not.

We played some games to start off the session. I especially liked the one that encouraged tolerance of other people's cultures. We were divided into two groups, one was sent outside and the other remained in the room. One group would be a tribe of people that did not believe in being too gregarious; they did not like to touch, look directly in the eyes or speak loudly. The other group was exuberant; they liked to speak loudly, to touch and feel and to be all up in your face when they talked. The two groups met and it was chaos. They stopped us after a few minutes and got some feedback on what each group thought of the other, based on the behavior. The comments were quite revealing. The quiet group was thought to be cold, selfish and uncivilized. The other group was described as aggressive, loud and vulgar. All this time, they were just being the harmless products of their different cultures.

This exercise was used to introduce and illustrate the cultural differences in U.S. classroom management. They gave some useful tips on effective teaching strategies. Members of staff and an alumnus provided tips on classroom management and discipline in the U.S.A. classroom. I got the feeling that she had taught at the elementary level. She was saying things that were practical at that level: wearing different hats for different days of the week and little things like that. She also spent an inordinate amount of time hinting at her displeasure with the salary at the time. I also suspected that the example of misconduct that they demonstrated was on the tame side. I was attentive throughout and was thinking of other ways of handling those misdemeanors. The important thing was to learn the rules, procedures and consequences as practiced by the particular school district as that varied throughout the country.

Since I had a two-hour drive ahead of me and we seemed to have covered the essential, I asked to leave. Before I left, I gave Dr. Johns, and some of the others I had spoken with, their thank you cards. The Program Team also gave us a card. Donna had asked for a ride, so we gathered our things, said our goodbyes and headed out. The rain was easing up at that point because it had done its thing while we were inside. Donna and I were pleased to have met again after all these years and began to make plans.

"Miss Wright, you know that we could even share a house since we're going to the same area." There is nothing I can do to get her to call me anything other than Miss Wright.

"That's a very good idea. We could save on rent and could even share car, since we'll be at the same school. I heard that you can get cars more cheaply from other dealers."

"Really, so how would we do this?"

"One of us could buy the car from them and the other could take on some of the other expenses until we are settled, then we would get another car and start splinting all expenses."

"That makes sense because I have my student loan to pay back and anything that I can save will help."

"I don't really have a lot of expenses, but I would like to retire from the everyday classroom by the time I am forty-five. When I finish this stint and my Masters, I want to run my own show."

"You go, Miss Wright. That is a good idea. I can hardly wait to pay off this loan and then be free. She did say she will call on Wednesday, right?"

"Yes. That was what she said. She seemed sincere enough, so I hope it is not one of those – don't call us, we'll call you—affairs.

She gave us her personal email, so what can I say? We'll just have to wait and see, won't we?"

"Yes, I suppose. What we can do is keep in touch, since we may be at the same school."

"I'm really thrilled at the prospect of both of us ending up at the same school teaching English. Imagine how we can share ideas and plan some exciting lessons together! You know that I want to learn Spanish though, so you may get to teach me in turn after all."

"The more we talk about this the more exciting it's getting. I can't wait to leave Norman Manley. Can you believe that I am finishing my degree this year?"

"I am very happy for you. I think this whole thing will be interesting, if nothing else."

We chatted about that and other matters of little or no importance until we arrived at her stop. We left wishing each other all the best as we settled in for the wait and for Wednesday to arrive.

CHAPTER SIX

From Interview to Departure

I am not about to torture you with the details of our wait for that call on the Wednesday. It never came. I took the liberty of sending a kind reminder to the email address I was given, but there had been no acknowledgement from the provider to indicate it was ever received. Isn't it funny how when you are on the dependent side you are expected to play by the rules, but those in authority can make and break them as they go? I believe that people should be treated with respect at every level and that being gracious to others is a reflection on you. The point is, you never know when and where you will meet again so make the little effort to leave a good impression and a nice taste with those you have the pleasure of meeting.

Credit to the team; they never let up. There were regular correspondences and there was an obvious effort to reassure us. There was pressure on me too because I needed to resign or apply for leave. I did not want to leave my job without another one in plain sight. There was another experience that I was looking forward to as well. I had applied to the CXC Board to work as an Assistant Examiner and I was offered the opportunity to go. I was excited about the prospect of grading exams. Since I had been teaching for so many years and was doing quite well, I thought it was a good idea to see what they were really looking for. I often predicted the passes well, but there were sometimes a surprise or two. The new course I was teaching at the sixth form level was especially surprising. I should have been pleased with the result— one hundred percent passing in the first year. I did not see some of those students passing. I wanted to be sure I understood what it was they were looking for so that I could become more focused in my teaching. The only person conducting workshops was Dr. Mac. These were very informative and helped the students to feel confident in what I was doing with them, since I would take them to the workshops.

It was not long before I received news that another school was interested in my profile. This was also from the State of North Carolina. I went online and did my research on the school. It was a secondary school and it was not in the major city, which is right up my street. I was thinking that students in the rural area would be receptive to a new teacher and curious about a new culture. If that kind of readiness were there, then a third of my work would be done. Donna had been provided information on the same school, so it was clear that, if we were successful, it was going to be Bertie County and not Vance.

My friend, Marie, was completing her first year on the Program and she was located in Vance County. We were making all kinds of plans when we thought I was going to Vance. We had gone to college together; that was where we met. She had done Math and English, but she has chosen to forget that English was her major. We had had some wonderful times together. She was one of the few friends with whom I shared my special place by the

Black River Sea. When life got to me I would go there and sit and watch the waves as they rolled in and things would always come back in perspective. Even when I was in college, I would take the bus for forty miles just to sit by the sea. It helped me to maintain my peace of mind and keep it in one piece—whole.

Every summer I would visit Marie in Kingston sometimes staying with her for the District Convention of Jehovah's Witnesses before we returned to St. Elizabeth. She loved the wide-open space at my house and the sense of freedom she got. We would always journey to Black River to my favorite place, but first we would stop in Middle Quarters to buy a pound of freshly done peppered shrimp. In Black River we would go by the bakery and buy some coco-bread hot out of the oven, freshly cut cheese, fruit juice and water. We would then take a leisurely walk down to the little cove. There we would spend the rest of the day sitting on rocks in the shade of the wild grape trees, moving only to throw stones in the waves or to be more comfortable. We talked a little, but contemplated a lot. You would never believe how refreshing it was! We were there together, but in our own little worlds.

When she called to let me know she was on the program, I was already chest deep in the application process. We discussed the possibility of sharing accommodations until I was established. Having spent so much time together over the years I knew I could share with her for awhile. We were both disappointed when that did not come through. I got some great laughs at her expense though. She was trying to tell me why it was best for me to visit her.

"Margery, you must come look fi me you hear?"

"Yes, but you will visit too, right?"

"No me dear, me fraid fi drive. Make me tell you what happen to me. Margery, me a go tell you, but don't laugh, you hear? When me come me rent a car. Me say, me just drive out a de car rental place when me hear—Bum!"

"What happen?" She was telling me, but I could hardly wait to hear and could hardly ask through the laughter that was bobbling in my mouth.

"Me say man, one car no lick me in a me back!'

"How you mean—just lick you in a you back?"

"A man did a drive. Him say him tink me did a go, go through the light. So him no do nottin' but stop in me back. Me have fi drive wid me trunk tie up fi bout two weeks. Den me dear, when me buy my car, bout two weeks me did have it for when one day me at my place, no have noting fi do so me decide to take a ride. Me a tell you the truth Margery, me slow down at a lickle circle in the road. Me look in all direction— No vehicle in sight. When me drive off me just hear BOOM!"

By this time I could hardly contain myself with laughter. She was a very good story teller and her tone was caught between wanting to laugh and cry. She spoke in a whisper as though someone else may be near her and she didn't want them to hear. Even her half-laugh was subdued, but I was wiping my eyes as I tried to imagine the scene.

"Marg, don't laugh, is a serious matter. Me dear, when me come out of the car and look pon de car, the two door dent up! You know say me have to pay to replace the doors."

"So what happen to it, den?"

"Me say, me no tell you—me can't drive! A wa me say? Me can't drive! What you tink me do? There was a pole in the middle of the road and I didn't do a thing, but drive right into it."

I wiped my eyes and tried to regain my composure, feeling sorry for her, I promised I would visit her if and when I got to the States. When I heard about the interest in Bertie county I started to make enquiries about where it was in relation to Vance. One of the responses I got was that it was near the sea. Imagine that! I made sure to get a new sketchpad and some water color paints. I thought that since I was so busy in Jamaica I was unable to indulge in my hobbies so this was a chance to get back to normal.

That night before the interview I made sure to jot down the questions I wanted to ask, and put my notes in my bag. This was going to be a mutual interview and I wanted to be alert so I decided to go to bed early. I was still not sleeping well. This was a residue from the time the house was burglarized the year before. I understand why it is said that ignorance is bliss. I had the funny feeling for some time that someone was gaining access to the house at nights. There was a Peeping Tom; I had seen one at my window some years before. There was that time when I came back from vacation and found that my desk had been ransacked. There were nights when I felt a presence in my room and felt a bright light on my face through the blanket over my head. I would close my eyes and wait for it to go away and it did. In the dark I would lie and wonder whether I had imagined the whole experience. When I was in England, one of my tenants called me to tell me that her cell phone had disappeared from the house, so we speculated that someone must have come in the house and removed it, but we were hesitant to draw a conclusion. When he came the year before, he had already removed some handbags and a laptop from the study before we knew we had company. Thankfully, he only took some phone cards and the money from a bag, but left everything else in the garage.

That night before the interview, I was asleep when I heard the sounds in the unfinished part of the house. At first I thought that it was a stray cat, but uncovered my head to listen more keenly. It was strange that a cat could get in, since the windows and doors were closed. I got up and switched on the light hoping to chase it away and the sound stopped. I turned off the light and went back to bed. The sound began again and then I saw the flashlight moving quickly around then it was off. Now what cat is going to take its own flashlight to see in the dark? I got up again, with my heart pounding, I turned on the lights and it was then that I noticed that the outer door was wide open. Without thinking I opened the door from the section of the house where I was and went out in the garage. I was mad! When I checked the outer part of the building where the sound was, I discovered that five gallons of paint and treatment for the wall had disappeared. I think that night I cursed at every thief that ever lived. My neighbors came, but there was nothing we could do.

It was not possible to sleep again. The police came and left with no positive word. When they had left I found a pair of pliers on the floor that did not belong to me, on my way to work, I took them to the police station. It was obviously left by the "visitor." They promised to call me as soon as they learned anything.

When I got to work, I used my non-contact period to make the call to Bertie. The principal was in a meeting so I told them who I was and left my number and a message. When my phone rang, I thought it was the police. My nerves were on edge. I was making the call from Liz's flat and contending with the barking fit of her neighbor's German shepherd and the blaring of a lawn mower outside.

It was the principal, Mrs. Burns returning my call. I was taken aback by the accent. I had seen her picture and knew that she was a woman of color. The tone I was hearing was not the sound I usually associated with African-Americans. That southern drawl is usually reserved for other people. Her voice was calming and reminded me of Donna Brazile; they even look alike. I apologized for the background noise and told her where I was and why. I was a little rattled and though I did not wish to make excuses sometimes it's good to know the condition of the playing field.

We went through the usual opening questions and she gave me a synopsis of her school and their goal.

"Miss Wright, we are currently going through some changes and especially with our grade nine group. We have started a new system which allows us to give more attention to that group."

"Yes. I got that from your website. I suppose you got your theme from this thrust: Redesigning for Excellence. How is this program organized?"

"We are going to have a different structure for these students in the STEM school. This is really an acronym for Science, Technology, English and Mathematics. So we hope to focus on those subject areas. We really need on board, teachers who are able to get results especially in the area of Writing."

"Well, I would guess that this is where I come in. We have a similar system to yours. Our grade nine over the years has been an area for concern because, I suppose, this is the middle of nowhere. It is a similar place as puberty—they are neither junior nor senior, so they are often more confused. Our Education Ministry is also trying something new to improve students' performance. We now have the Reform of Secondary Education Curriculum and I am proud to have been a part of it."

"What is involved in this program?"

"It employs the thematic approach to teaching writing and the other skills. There is something else which makes it practical. This is a technical high school which makes it a good thing for making the teaching learning process practical, keep in mind that this is our aim as educators. The students have practical areas, such as auto mechanic, home economics, food and nutrition, wood work, metal work, agriculture among others. As a teacher of English I am able to integrate those subjects in the content. This idea is also endorsed by the HEART Trust, which is a government-funded organization that supports the technical schools plan for education."

"Uhaa? Okay, that sounds good? We have a State Writing Test each year and our school has not been doing as well as we would like in this area. One of our goals is to boost these scores among our grade ten students."

"I'd like to think that this is my area of specialization. Over the years, I've had very good results in this area. Let me tell you one of the things I've done. Each year I observe my students in grade nine and invite some of them to sit the English exam when they're in grade ten. The London-based exam is more writing and comprehension while the Caribbean-based exam is more comprehensive and literary based. Usually, if they have an A or B in the GCSE it is good for any transcript and this allows them to do another subject at grade eleven if they want to do so, including English. Over the years we have maintained a high pass rate, especially among students who would not have qualified to sit CXC English."

"Uhaa? That's very good." After she told me some more about the goals of the school how they plan to achieve them and how I could contribute, we spoke a little about the government's initiative for "No Child Left Behind." I told her I was aware of the Bush initiative and told her about the similar policy in Jamaica, where we say, "Every child can learn; every child must learn." In this discussion I was able to establish how I provide for children with special needs. She got some more information about my suitability, and then it was my turn to ask questions.

"Please tell me a little about the staff turnover rate at your school?" I asked. I know that this can be indicative of the climate at the school.

"Well, I am new to this school; I've just come here last year. But since I have been here, it has not been bad."

"I see. There is the suggestion in that statement that it had been bad at some point. What do you suppose has contributed to this turnover?"

"I think the fact that this area is not near the city?" This is not a question it's just part of her inflection, or perhaps her uncertainty.

"Some people prefer to be in the city." I was not sure if it was the truth, but I think it was plausible.

"Well, that won't be a problem for me. I like country. It's the main reason that I have opted for this area." We spoke a bit more before we finished the interview. I felt good about it, considering that this was a long distance telephone interview and we were on the phone for almost an hour. I was pleased. I liked her; she was easy to talk to and seemed sincere about wanting the school to do well.

A few days later, one of the vice principals from my school, came in the staff room grinning from ear to ear. He said something to me that seemed cryptic at the time, but later he told me what he meant. Apparently, he was the member of admin Mrs. Burns had called to confirm that I was all that I claimed to be. He was telling the others that I was gone. They were all aware of my plans, because there were evaluation forms that they had to fill out. All indications showed that I was bound for Bertie, wherever that was.

Suddenly, everything was moving at warp speed. On the eleventh of June, I was informed of Bertie County's interest in my file; by the twelfth, I had done the interview; by the thirteenth, I had received my job offer; by the nineteenth, my employment was confirmed; and by the twentieth, the placement package was on its way. In the meantime, things were getting hectic at work. Exams had to be written, vetted, printed, stapled and administered. I had accepted the offer to be a marker for Communication Studies exams, so I was making plans to travel to Kingston for two weeks to grade papers. I started grading my internal exams and working on my report forms. I was really burning the candle at both ends.

My timetable had gotten lighter because the grade elevens and sixth formers were sitting their external exams. Technically, they had finished with school so that allowed me to focus on the grades nine and ten. They were completing their internal papers and already the deadlines for grade submission had been posted. I made sure to take my exam papers with me so that at the end of the day I could continue with my grading. For the first two nights we stayed at a teachers' college. That campus was something else. Everything on it was outstanding: the mangoes were big and yellow as if you could see the juice in them. The lizards, mosquitoes and roaches were also big, but scared the daylights out of me. The water was off by nine at nights. It's not that I don't love nature and all that, but I don't want to get so close to realize my appreciation. I did not keep that accommodation.

It was difficult to get the hang of the grading system initially, but we soon got in a rhythm. By this time I was grading external during the day and internal papers at night. There were eight of us at our table and we bonded very quickly. Karen, the marker to my right, thought I was a curious character. Every now and again she would marvel at something else.

"Marjorie, you ever get angry? I mean really angry!"

"Of course, a few nights ago a thief came to my house and I surprised myself. He was gone when I got outside, but I really ranted." You know that the others at the table were very amused. What would I have done if I had seen him?

"But hear you though—you're too calm. Even when you talk about it, you still don't sound like you could get angry." My experience reminded everybody of some burglary incident, but

I think Jessica related the most interesting account. She said, "One of our teachers—in fact, she teaches English too—went home one night and, apparently she was very tired, so she just went to bed. She woke up when she heard a sound like there was someone in her bedroom. When she opened her eyes, she saw a man standing in her bedroom, looking down at her. Still groggy from sleep and a little confused she asked: 'Who are you?' And the thief responded, 'I is a tief!' She said, 'No, no, no, it's not I *is a tief*, it's I *am* a thief!'"

By this time we were in stitches, but the story was not finished. Jessica continued, "Of course the thief became angry, so he was like, 'Look, woman, if you never lef de key in a de door me wouldn't come in a you house fi teif. As a matter of fact, take you key and next time, lock you door.' And he threw down the key and left. When she got up and went to the living room, it was empty— all her furniture and appliances were missing! When the police came, they found the things stolen, stacked in the ally. She is truly a teacher, teaching anybody anytime, even a burglar." We all had a good laugh at that one.

By this time I had men working at my house to install burglar bars. That was the least I could do, ensure that my loved ones staying on at the house would be safe. The money I earned from marking went right into paying off the welders. I wanted to be sure that I was not in debt to anyone at this point, so I was making every effort to not incur new expenses and to clear those that had arisen. I wanted to be in a position where I owe my friends only love.

Donna and I were keeping in contact, since she too had been offered a position as teacher of English at Bertie. Our plans were still on. Since we were both staying on the university campus, we saw each other when I was in Kingston for the grading period. When I finished grading the internal exam papers I had more time to complete some of the assignments in the online package, but I was not getting as many done as I would have liked. We had received our packages with further instructions and were awaiting more news on the visa appointment. In the mean time we were continuing our collection of things Jamaican that we could use to dispense the culture.

On July four I received my first email from the local advisor. It was a welcome and all you need to know letter. The information was useful. On the sixth we had information for the visa appointment because there were some inconsistencies on my form; it had to be sent back to the States. On the nineteenth, I learned that the appointment was set for the third of August. By the twenty-third, there was a note from the local advisor urging the recipient to make a decision on housing and furniture. Some people were moving on and selling their furniture at a reasonable price and another was willing to rent a part of her house and share her kitchen appliances. The house had its own washer and drier and the lady was said to be "mature, quiet and easy to get along with." Donna and I discussed the information we were receiving, but we were unable to decide since we did not really have a clear idea of what was a good deal. We held off on making any decision.

On the twenty-seventh, I received another note concerning my visa appointment. The correct form had been sent to me and I had gathered the rest of the document I needed to be presented at the embassy.

"So Marj, how are the plans going? I've not been seeing you much since the other day, you very busy, man!" Liz was serious about being kept informed.

"Yea, I have to go to the embassy on the third of August. Can you believe that I have found a buyer for the car?"

"Really? That's good. You see how the Lord works out things?"

"I've learned to rely on him even more as these blocks are removed. The girl who is buying the car is willing to wait until I am ready to leave. As a matter of fact, when I go up to Kingston on the third, I'll just leave the car."

"Marj, you know me a go miss you though."

"But you must, I would be disappointed if you didn't." We both laughed.

"Boy, Marj, you not easy you know—you not easy at all."

"Guess what, I will be sharing house with Donna. You remember her? She did Spanish, so you should know her. The funny thing is she majored in English and Spanish. I hope now that I will have more time I can learn Spanish."

"Listen, I don't want to hear anything about you and Spanish. Marj, Marj, how long you suppose to be learning Spanish? And why you stop? No tengo ni idea!"

"That's not fair, claro que si, tengo muy busy-!" That was as far as I got. We both collapsed in laughter when I attempted my Spanglish. I was surely going to miss these moments.

Tac also wanted to know how things were. She had different concerns. "So, Margery, how things going, me dear? You find out where you going yet?" Both Liz and Tac may ask the same questions, but they will have different interests.

"I know it is North Carolina and that it is a high school in Bertie, which is supposed to be in the rural area. I've heard that it is near the sea. I asked Brother Georges about the congregations in those parts so he gave me the Societies number. I will try to call before I leave."

"Okay, once you find the brothers, it should help you to settle in quickly. Den the money good? Some of those agencies no pay good, you know."

"Let me show you the pay package and you can do the math. You know though Tac, I just want enough to take care of my expenses. More than anything, I want some time away."

"Let me see it." She looked at it. "But you stay well, girl. If me did a get this… He-hey!" She did one of her laughs again. "Go on ya me dear." That was her vote of confidence.

The interview at the embassy was different in many ways. There was a new embassy building in a different part of town and the fact that I was supported, gave me confidence. Donna should have met me there so I went and joined the ever present long line. To make matters worse, it was raining that day. When Donna arrived, I told her to join me in the line. I was just so excited to see her, I was not thinking of the implication of my action.

Shortly afterward, we saw another teacher who was also going to Bertie and invited him over too. We knew this was wrong and someone didn't fail to tell me how wrong it was. Incidentally, she was also a teacher for the program. I apologized and offered to change position with her, but she refused, she merely wanted to make her point. There were no delays. We went through the different check points and were asked a few questions of little or no relevance as the personnel went through the motion of an interview. It was slam-dunk!

The hurdles came with my quest to sell the car. By now you have an opinion of Emperor's temperament. I was trying to make sure that everything was in good working order because I was selling it to a woman, if it was being sold to a man I probably would not have bothered so much. I took the car to the mechanic and had everything checked. During the check up the car developed a strange knocking sound. No mechanic could locate or silence it. The car drove, the air condition worked, but the sound persisted to my embarrassment. After trying to get the price reduced to far below its value, the lady decided that she would not buy it. When she made her decision, I was still in Kingston. It was getting very late and I wanted to leave Kingston before dark, so I took it back to the car parts dealer who had sold me the engine.

If I had the original paper for the used engine I could have sold it in St. Elizabeth because there were many people who were interested in buying it. I was able to speak to the owner on the phone, but he still had not located the original papers. His brother offered to buy the car, since he bought and sold cars. I was tired of the whole thing and agreed to sell way below the value. I was happy and nervous. This is Kingston you know, one of the world's highest murder rate in a country that is not at war. How was I going to go Down Town at that time of the evening with so much money in my possession? When we sat down to count the money he said he was paying a portion and would pay the rest by the Wednesday. Men! I didn't quarrel. I reasoned that, if they robbed me, it would only be a portion of the money, so if I was not killed in the process, I could use the cash to start to settle my affairs. I knew the family in another setting so I knew he could not evade me and not pay the balance so I agreed. I drew up a sales agreement and had Donna witnessed it, as well as another man who worked at the shop. I counted my loss and headed home. I needed to take two thousand US dollars for my resettlement so I lodged the money and made my request for the money at the bank. I used the rest to complete some work at my house as I had to make my house comfortable for those who were going to stay there and for the hurricane season.

"Miss Wright, you did get the email about buying a car when you get there?" Donna wanted to know.

"Yes, they certainly know how to pressure people. When it's expressed like that we don't have much of a choice, do we?"

"You right. So let me see if I get this. We can rent, lease or buy. But they want you to let them know what we are doing, right?"

"Basically, but notice how we are not left with a lot of choices—look how attractive their package is made to seem. Marie said that it works out to be expensive. You still want us to just get one car to start?"

"Yes, yes, Miss, that makes more sense 'cause I don't have no money."

"Aright, let's do it. What about the house, are we still on to share?"

"Yes, remember that we told the local advisor and ting… so we are ready."

"OK, so it seems like we are set then. Let's keep in touch."

So things were going according to plan. I had to get on the case of the car dealer when he wanted to put off the balance of the payment. Karen would have been proud of me. When I was finished, he said the money would be in the account by twelve and it was there. Some people just don't know when to stop! On the seventh of August, there was another urgent message for a final decision on the car.

"Miss Wright, they say if we don't take the car now, we can't get the same terms later and I think I want to take it. Brian said it's best if I take it now." Donna was getting worried. Brian her boyfriend was already in the States.

"Aright, no problem, so we each will buy our own car from them then. Where are you getting your connecting flight?"

"I'm going to Houston and you?"

"I'm going to Miami. So I suppose we'll see each other in Raleigh. Well, take care until then."

The next few days were very hectic. All the parties were out of the way. I went around and said my goodbyes. I was making sure all my legal affairs and businesses were taken care of and arrangement was made for my transportation to the airport. My suitcases were packed and I was ready. This was the hurricane season, so I could not be too careful.

August thirteen was the big day—or was it? It did not have that ring or that drum roll quality at all. After the parties, the expressions of love and the rest, it was an anticlimax. I went to the airport with a stranger. As we drove through the town, I watched the faces of the people as they went about their business. Nobody knew I was leaving to the unknown; nobody cared. Like an epiphany, the move suddenly seized me. I suddenly realized that I was as dispensable to this world as anything else. It simply chews you up then spits you out—like juiceless gum—if there is anything left to spit out.

CHAPTER SEVEN

Arrival in the US - The Dream and the Reality

There is such a thing as over anticipation and I was suffering from a mild case of it. I had worked up until the twelfth hour and I still felt deep, deep down inside that I was going for a significant and meaningful change. My arrival in Miami was forgettable. Except for the monotony of answering the questions I already answered on the form, the only bright spot was meeting several other teachers who were also arriving for the program. After we collected our luggage and checked them for the other leg of the journey, we assembled in the departure lounge. There were about six of us, plus one young man who was going to South America to study for a year. Megan was in the group. (You'll remember that she was the teacher of Spanish.) They had a lot to talk about because she had gone to Columbia as well for part of her study. Except for Megan, I was meeting everybody else for the first time and she along with June and Angela were also bound for Bertie.

The rest of us soon brought our weight to bear on the conversation and so the talk turned to the matter of our move and what we were expecting to gain from it. The different groups of the society were represented. Megan was divorced and had her

Masters degree in Spanish. June was still married and specialized in Food and Nutrition. Angela was married with children and her area was Elementary Education. Mrs. Robinson was a more mature woman, married with grown children. Her husband would be staying in Jamaica. Carl was divorced with children and had a child on the way from a new relationship. I was the single one in the group and, by now, you are familiar with my circumstances.

Oh, to listen to the plans and dreams of this aspiring group! A better way of life was the recurring theme. Everybody seemed to see this as their last opportunity, and fastest way to fulfill their dreams. I would later come to understand fully the concept of the American dream. There were plans for the mates and children to follow, plans to buy land or build on what they already had in Jamaica or to buy and resettle in the States. Again I thought to myself that this was really my "me time." I had no husband or children coming. I was not saving to build or buy a house. I really just wanted a situation that was not as stressful as the one I was leaving. I wanted to be in a position where I had access to some technology to enhance my instruction and to increase enjoyment of both the students and myself in the classroom. In addition, I had promised my superiors at home that I would see what works in these education systems in the first world and share with them in order to improve our system. Lastly and most significantly, I wanted to grow spiritually.

Because I had eaten late in the afternoon and had a snack on the plane, I decided to not sniff too deeply when some of the others bought food at the food court. I had had to pay one hundred dollars for one of my cases at the Montego Bay Airport in Jamaica. The bag contained the teaching aids I had packed and which I hoped will be worth the trouble. I was not ready to continue to deplete what little funds I had brought with me. There was food in my case too, so if I was hungry when I get to the hotel, I could address that matter then.

We landed in Raleigh about ten at night. By the time we cleared customs, there was a team waiting for us. They verified who we were, welcomed us and gave us the itinerary. We carried our bags to the outside where we would take the shuttle to the hotel. Angela and I got on the second trip. What I found curious and unsettling was that nobody so far had been able to say where Bertie is located, some people had never even heard of the place—interesting!

When we arrived we checked in, got our phone card and keys, did the preliminaries and then went in search of our room. Angela and I were assigned the same room. We didn't mind at all. We got our snack and went to make our one phone call. I was not able to get my mother, so I called Erica, my sister in New York, so she could pass on the news that I had landed and that I was alive and well. After our calls, we set about finding the thermostat. That room was cold! It was not until late the following afternoon that I found it.

"Angela, did you select one of the flats as yet? The ones the local advisor wrote about…" I asked.

"No, you know, as a matter of fact, I am not sure if I am going to be in the same area as you people. Did you select any?"

"No, but there is a girl, Donna, you probably met her. We are thinking of sharing a house. I think it is a good idea; we'll both be at the same school—teaching the same subject. We can plan our lessons together and all that."

"That's great! You can even car pool sometimes. I think I would've loved that. I will need a house though because my children will be coming later."

"I understand. I hope it won't be hard to find somewhere before we have to start school."

"My dear, I certainly hope so."

Over the next couple of days, we went through quite a few activities: opening checking accounts, making our down payment on the car, signing up for insurance, attending different sessions and going on the road to prove that we could drive on the right side of the road. This latter activity was an interesting challenge. I must confess that it provided me with a lot of laughs too. As you try to imagine this episode, keep in mind that the driver is on the left side of the road in Jamaica. You have watched people who have thrown a bowling ball or a golfer who has made a putt, as the ball nears the target they lean with it willing it to hit the target or go into the hole, as if by leaning themselves they can influence the direction of the missile. I felt much the same way as Angela was driving.

Joe, the instructor, led us to his car. It is a big black one that reminds me of the Lincolns used as taxis in New York. I decided to watch and learn, so Angela took the wheels and I took the back seat. The Program required that you should be driving for at least two years. Some people were planning to drive for two years and some had had their licenses for two years. Regardless of the situation, the problem was in proving that we could drive on the other side of the road. I will spare Angela's name and not tell you about her driving, but just to say she had to drive a second time.

I, on the other hand was something else. It was my turn to drive after Angela pulled into a service station and parked. I wiped the sweat from my palm and headed to the driver's seat. I adjusted the seat and mirrors and was ready. I told myself to do this thing like the doctors in surgery, just talk myself through.

"Okay Marjorie, I want you to turn right and drive straight ahead." Joe said as I breathed out like I was about to take a plunge in some icy water.

"Turn right and drive straight." I told myself, "So, put on the right indicator." The next thing I knew the windscreen wipers were flashing like a lover's hand at the airport's waving gallery. So I had to learn that the controls were on the other hand. I had gone through the road signals, because some of them were different from what I was used to at home. I managed to get through driving around the city and soon I was on the highway.

"Marjorie, I see that you are used to driving on the highways. Now speed up a bit; you are going to merge. Good, good—now merge. Wow! That was good. Did you do a lot of driving in Jamaica?"

"Yes, I had to drive every day. And I went into the city often, this meant going on the highway and merging too."

"It shows. You drive very well. " he said, but he spoke too soon.

He almost changed his mind when we returned to the hotel. I turned in the driveway that leads to the parking lot and I took up residence on the left side. After I had done so well out in the town and on the highway, I came back and was totally confused. Angela was telling me to get back on the right and Joe was threatening to take back the compliment he had paid me--along with the points I had earned--and a car was coming at me. I don't know how I got back to the parking lot and parked that car, but I am glad I did. That was no cultural difference; it was more like a cultural cerebrovascular accident. For a moment, I felt as though the wires in my brain were all knotted.

"Well, Marjorie, you amaze me. Where are you going to teach?"

"Bertie, do you know where that is?"

"Oh yes, it is—where is it? Oh yes, it is in the hills."

"Really, I heard it was near the sea. So far nobody has been able to tell me where this place is located. Are you sure that it even exists?" We spoke a little about how the State was divided in many small counties and the size made it difficult to know the location of some of these smaller counties.

The next man we met was not as pleasant as Joe. He congratulated me and gave me a little object to clip on the visor for glasses and proceeded to berate Angela. I have never heard an adult speak like that to another except maybe in the movies. We quickly left his presence. That sort of negative energy can do severe damage. He obviously did not like himself and was projecting it on others. How can somebody be so unkind to a complete stranger?

The bag we received when we arrived was filling up fast. There were a lot of goodies and I was guessing that the other sessions we were attending would prove to be helpful when we got in the school. I had one question after I had noticed a peculiar pattern in the presentations. There were all these things about what we should do. It was beginning to feel that there were all these Dos and Don'ts and I was starting to see my little power slipping away. I asked the burning question: How much autonomy, if any, does the teacher have in the classroom? The person to whom the question was directed went around and around and I am still waiting for an answer. I got from his circumlocution that because this is a litigious society, there was only so much that the teacher could do—which was very little!

The night before we left there was a party, dinner and dance. I danced and made the acquaintance of our youngest guest. He was about nine years old and we talked a little. It must have made an impression on him because he made me a lovely card while he was in day care. Unfortunately the card went missing. I really felt sad about it because the day they were leaving he would not leave until he found me to give me that card. The mother was very relieved to see me because their ride had arrived and he was insisting on giving me the card himself. I still think about him. I would have loved to know how he was adjusting to the new environment and school. I still hope to see him one of these days.

"Marjorie, guess what? My car will be here for me." Angela was aglow, grinning from ear to ear.

"You mean someone is taking your car here, so you won't be traveling with us?"

"That's right. I will get to see my car now." She had passed her driving test and I was glad that she had this boost to her ego.

This would prove to be a very significant gesture because she was given a guided tour and driving tips by her driver.

The rest of us, who were going to Bertie, went in a minivan. We were chatting animatedly as we went. Somewhere along the way the talk rolled around to housing. Someone mention that they heard that there were three flats.

"Which two people are sharing?" June wanted to know.

"Donna and I are sharing?"

Donna was quiet for awhile. Then she said, "Miss Wright, ___ ahm, I not going to share again."

"Oh? And when were you going to tell me this? I mean, this is something of a surprise."

I could have made my own arrangements, but I thought that this was mutually beneficial. She didn't have much to say. Basically, her boyfriend had said it would be best if she didn't have a housemate as he was planning on being a regular visitor. This did not put me off for long. I am not a worrier. When one door closes, another entrance or exit can be found or created. I would jump that hurdle when I got to it.

The local advisor and the cars were all waiting when we got to the county office. The most memorable part of that day is the sight of the seven Mitsubishi Lancers all in a row—charcoal grey, silver, sand grey, and blue. When we drove out it was like a motorcade on the road to Williamston in Martin County. We got to the apartments without incident.

"Marjorie, I could have told you that she was going to do that. So what're you going to do now? You think it is because you spoke to her about her dress?" Angela was trying to be encouraging.

"I don't think it could have been that. Even she must have noticed that those clothes were too skimpy for this crowd. I am not doing anything. Just watch and see how things will work out for my good."

"Marjorie, what're you talking about?" Angela was looking at me as if she suddenly realized that I had antlers or antenna instead of ears.

"Angela, this is just one more test of my faith. I'm becoming used to this. Just when I seem to have my ducks all in a row, something goes wrong and I have to change angle, but I still get all of them. Just watch and see what happens."

"Girl, you not easy. I would not take it like that. So you letting her get the flat too?"

"Yes, if she wants it."

"Girl, you're really something else. And you see how she just jump up and take it without even asking you if you did want it, after a she change her mind! Well, some people…"

"Well, look at it this way; it's a case that Jesus wins again—the Golden Rule—because I would love for someone to make the same sacrifice for me I am making for her. Angela, Christianity and love is not something I talk about; it's a way of life; it's what I do. But you'll see how it works out fine."

By this time two other teachers had arrived. Marilyn and Janice came by to see the latest arrivals. Angela and I were sitting on the stairway while the others who had selected their flats animatedly discussed their acquisitions. I did not have to wait long for my returns. As it turned out, Marilyn was the teacher who had the house to share--the house with the washer, drier, and mature woman willing to share kitchen and utensils. Since I was on my own now, that option was opened to me and I accepted. Before I would take up my position, there would be one more test. It occurred that night after we had bought our air beds and a few other necessities for temporary settlement. Megan and June decided that they were going to spend the night at the house that I had selected. While it is true that their apartments did not have electricity, they could have spent the night at the local advisor's house. I think that sometimes we should allow people a chance to do what is right. You should not always tell people how to act.

Angela had still not found a place and I thought it was good to stick with her and provide some support for her. She stayed by the Advisor's flat and I stayed by Donna's flat. We inflated our beds and slept as best as we could under the circumstances. Carl was in one room; Donna and I were in the other, on our recently acquired air beds.

The next day we went to a meeting with the representatives from the county office. They gave us some basic ideas about how the school system operates and invited us to sign up for payment of our salaries for twelve or ten months. We also signed up to join the credit union. I was making sense of this whole thing. "One hand washes the other." My future housemate made a presentation about how she established her routine and enforced discipline in her classroom. She was a teacher at the middle school. According to her and some others present, these were tried-and-proven behavior management methods. I was becoming concerned about the amount of activities that must take place before actual teaching can go on. I was wondering if these students were really so unaware of why they are in the classroom that precious time has to be spent on these areas of conduct every day. Hmmm! The locals were very amused by our intolerance of the air conditioning.

There was quite a fanfare to mark our arrival. We were taken on a tour of the Hope Plantation and Great House. I found this tour to be very informative. It helped me to develop a greater sense of appreciation for the Native Americans and their survival skills. We were given an incentive to return and take two other people. How lovely it would be to take my students there as a reward for performing or for behaving well in class! This was something I did one year in Jamaica. I saved and asked friends for contributions until I could cover the cost for the top ten most outstanding performers. They were very encouraged by it and continued to do well after this gesture. This experience made me think of doing it for these students in the States.

We went on a boat ride along the Cashie River. What can I say? I was relieved to be back on land. Not even the Black River can be compared to the water in that river. It was murky. To this day I seriously doubt that there was anything living in that body of water. Yet there is a regular boating business going on this river. Angela was considering it to be one of the activities her children could engage in when they arrived. Not far from this area there was a Mini Zoo. Later I would understand how important these areas of interest are to this otherwise pedestrian place. An area where I could easily pass the day was the small art gallery. I was hoping to spend many quiet days meandering through this little shop. Our last stop was at the council building. Here we were joined by the judge, the realtor, sheriff, banker and basically everybody who was anybody in the community. Many promises of support were made. They expressed their gratitude for our sacrifice and made small talk as we partook of the local delicacies that were prepared as part of our initiation in the community. We received more bags filled with mementos, business cards and stationery. I was hoping that this affair was not merely for show, but that they were serious about wanting to help us to help their young. As I listened to them talk, I wondered whether these children were aware of how much money, time and planning was going into them. For their sakes, I hoped that they were conscious of it and that they valued it.

On the domestic front, we were quite active too. We had attended a welcome party put on by the local advisor and the other teachers. We also got a tour of the local town of Williamston in Martin County; this was where most of us lived. This I learned later was wisdom of the ages. They warned us that we did not want to be living next to our students. By now you probably know that because of our African heritage, Jamaicans use a lot of proverbs in their conversations. The proverb that would fit this situation is: Pig ask him mother, "Why you mouth so long?" the mother replied, "Me pickney, you a grow you will see." We would ask the other teachers,

"Why is it so bad to live next to these students?" and they would say:

"Humm, you'll soon see."

The local advisor also had a folder with information, fliers and brochures for us. Now you can just imagine the collection of binders, books, magazines, brochures and manuals we had accumulated since we landed. As I looked on the greenery along the road as we drove through the country roads, I thought to myself, "Forestry, your days are numbered." Was it necessary to have all these papers? Already I was suffering from information overload. What was the point of having all this information, if I would not have the time to read it? Later, it was agonizing to discover that some of those papers contained the same information from different sources. Immediately it occurred to me that there was a problem with communication.

From the information provided by the local advisor, I was able to call the Kingdom Hall. My housemate and I went in search of it. After losing our way several times, we asked a woman for directions. When we found it, I made a note to go there the following night. Angela accompanied me the Thursday and we lost our way going back. I began to panic when I saw the gas gauge flashing red. We were in separate cars, communicating on the phone. It was a relief to see the bowling alley. We turned around and headed back to the town. At nights the place takes on an eerie darkness and the pale street lights barely glow in the dark. Nowhere really stands out. Little wonder I got lost the first night I was going home alone. At one point I found myself going down the wrong way on a one way road at that. From my experience I can empathize with people doing some crazy things on the road. You never know—they could be used to driving on the other side of the road. I drove back to a point I recognized and started from there. Experiences like these helped me to find my way around as I grew in confidence and discovered the place.

My bedroom and bathroom were small, but they would prove to be my sanctuary. I inflated my bed and made it each day. I hung my clothes in the closet, because that was all I could do, and then placed my toiletries in the bathroom. The floor was to be my desk and shelf for a month or so. We learned early that it was not just money that bought things in the USA, but credit. The local advisor was kind enough to let us use her good name and address to purchase small items like cell phones within a certain price range. Then later she introduced us to the sales rep at a popular local furniture store. All this tiptoeing was because we were still waiting on our Social Security cards. We had to go to Washington in North Carolina to get this process under way. Social Security cards were needed for rentals and credit was needed to build a credit rating. A good credit rating opened other doors for you. I was learning fast. So, although I could have paid cash after my first pay check for the things I needed, I was encouraged to pay for it in installments and build my credit rating, because this is crucial in the United States.

I was unimpressed with how flimsy the furniture was, but then it was all a part of this disposable society. My first purchase was a bedroom set, which included a bed side table with two drawers, a chest of drawers and mirror. I also got a desk and a folding chair and a printer. Since I had a laptop, I was now open for business. The space left, after I had arranged everything, was about two feet from the door into the room between the desk and the drawers. This narrow passage led to the bed where it opened up by another foot or so and this little passage also went to the closet. The printer was positioned on the box from which it was taken and placed at the foot of the little desk. The books were on the floor to the right of the desk and propped up between the wall and the closet. This was to be my comfort zone for the next eight months.

Angela was still homeless, even after all of us had been housed. We would drive with her in search of a house when we were not at some meeting. These trips took us to Ahoskie, Windsor, and Colerain. Many times, she was on her own or making calls. I felt her frustration when she would return at the end of the day and still had no positive word. Part of the problem was that we were trying to maintain our standard of living accommodations as we had had in Jamaica or near those standards. There were many concerns about the conditions of some of the houses we saw. But it would have been difficult to live in Martin County and work in Colerain, so she needed to find some place close to work and convenient for her family.

She eventually found a house in Windsor. The house was one dark and forbidding place. The inside did not suggest that the architect was sure of what he wanted to do, so he had added or subtracted as he went along. The kitchen, for example, had no windows and was dark without the electricity. The living-room window was like an afterthought and the one in the bathroom had me praying that the neighbors were not peeping toms. There were dark brown ply board walls throughout the inside of the house and the ceiling was almost black. The battery in the smoke alarm needed changing and that thing beeped annoyingly all night. At one point I got a knife and a chair and attempted to unscrew it in order to stop the noise. It made such a piercing whistle as it protested loudly, that I decided to try and live with the beep—beep—beep which was a lot louder than a hospital monitor and a thousand times more disturbing.

I had found out all this when I went to spend the first night with her. I remember the first time I was moving into my own apartment in Jamaica, that Tac had come to spend the night and it was very reassuring. I thought Angela deserved company in that place—even if it was just the first night. Although I felt sorry for her as she went from one end of the state to another trying to get the utilities in place, I was even more proud of her. She didn't complain. Yes, she lamented the rigmarole to get basic needs like gas and light, but she was not the – "please feel sorry for me" kind of person. We called each other and talked about the obstacles, helped to strengthen each other's faith and thus endure together. There is always a way out when you have support.

CHAPTER EIGHT

First Day of School - The Culture Shock!

The first thing I saw when I entered the parking lot at the school, was the spanking football field, "Home of the Falcons." The aluminum seats glistened in the morning sun. The school itself was like a fortress when compared to the other buildings I had seen in the vicinity. The red bricks stood out bright against the otherwise green landscape. It was a flat structure with solid doors and reinforced windows. In some rooms the glass windows seem to go from ceiling to floor. The thought of how well lit those spacious classrooms would be almost made me dizzy with delight. Donna and I were eager to get started.

We attended our first meeting at the school. The first difference I noticed was that there was no invocation. Almost every meeting in Jamaica begins with songs and prayer. I was curious to see what else was different. From there on things went according to script—welcome, introductions, we received our classroom assignment and were encouraged to meet with our department chair. In the outset it was difficult to meet with this person. She was often going off to see to some family crisis. Her siblings were older and they were a close family, so she was called whenever they had a problem. While she was out, Ms. Luisa, a young teacher from the Philippines was very helpful to Donna and me.

After I saw Ms. Luisa's classroom, I could not wait to get to mine. She must have been working on that room for the entire summer. The room was not just a classroom. It was a haven for learning. There were plants, pictures, teaching aids, white board, green board, notice board, projector, computers, television and all sorts of other educational materials that I have always believed every viable classroom should have. The room was so neat that I could not expect anything, but the most esoteric activities taking place there.

"Ms. Wright, - a mean- you saw that room? Man, is so it neat!" Donna said.

"Donna, if anybody had told me a classroom could be so neat, I would say it's a lie. Now I can't wait to see my room and to start to fix it up too."

"Yeah man. You know we can set up a corner like she did there and call it our 'cultural corner,' no true?"

"I'm thinking—if we accomplished so much with so little at home; imagine how much we'll be able to do with all these things available to us!"

"You know! Did you find your room as yet? Mine is right down the hall in front of the main office."

"You want to walk with me? I was on my way, but just like how they didn't know where Bertie is nobody seems to know where in the school M08 is to be found. Let's go."

FIRST DAY OF SCHOOL - THE CULTURE SHOCK!

We were actually in the 300 building. When we got back to the 100 building, we encountered some of the other Jamaican teachers. They had found their classrooms too except for Megan who was told that she would be "floating" from class-to-class until the former Cosmetology room was converted. I decided to ask for directions from those who were there from the previous year. Tonetta, another Jamaican teacher who is also a teacher of English, came to my rescue.

"Which classroom are you looking for?"

"M08."

"Oh. We're going to share the same unit, so you can come with me."

I simply assumed that she meant that we would be teaching the same content and so we had the same unit plans. As we left the Foods Room together, we started chatting as we walked. We went through a double door marked EXIT and were out in the North Carolinian sunshine. I don't think I was really focused on the path as we left the secure brick building and approached some mobile structures at the back of the school. There was no perimeter fencing and the main road was a stone's throw from the mobile unit. A minor road, badly in need of repairs ran a few feet at the back door of the building and the window. As we neared the structure, I could see the wooden ramp that provided access to the two doors leading to Rooms M07 and M08. There was a wooden porch overlooking some stagnant water which had settled alongside the ramp like a moat. Was this really to be my classroom?

Clearing the cobwebs from the lock, I inserted the key. I turned right and the key spun around in the lock, but the door did not budge. I turned the key in the other direction, but there was still no positive response. After trying all the tricks, lifting and turning, pulling and twisting and pushing and turning without success, I went around to the back of the building to try the other door. Although this did not open on the first try, I was not put through all the paces as before. The door gave and we went in. Since the door was not keen to admit me, I wondered whether it was to protect me from what was inside or perhaps it was loath to admit the future.

We stood. We stared. We sniffed. It was the odor that made itself known. The room smelled like a wet dog. There must be some mistake. We tried to reconcile the scene before us with the memories of the rooms in the other buildings.

"Ms. Wright," Donna stopped and I understood. I too was having difficulty organizing my thoughts to express my feelings.

"Donna, are you seeing what I'm seeing?"

"Miss... well ahm, I mean..." she gave up trying to articulate what she saw.

Naturally, it was nothing like anything we had seen up to that point. The single green chalkboard was on the short wall to the front, flanked by the two doors. It was hardly visible from the front door because a small section was projecting into the room. This projection formed part of a smaller room which may have been intended for a toilet or kitchenette. The projection was about four feet and had a door in it. A grey, steel filing cabinet stood just inside of the back door and was partially hiding the board. Above the cabinet, affixed to the wall and ceiling was the ubiquitous television set. An old, scratched and chipped teacher's desk stood naked and forlorn between the chalkboard and the rest of the room. Combination desks and chairs for the students were strewn across the room. The floor was showing some signs of cracks and dirt. The walls would have been bare except for the right wall from the front door. Leaning against this wall was a dilapidated book shelf, which was falling apart under the weight of some very heavy and very old Spanish books. The wall to the front which ran behind the front door carried the old telephone. Upon closer inspection, I discovered that there was tape on it which was actually holding the receiver together. The far wall bore the old air condition unit and gave the impression that someone was trying to remove it by digging at the dry wall with a small tool on a daily basis. There was a window in the center of the back wall and one in the side above the old book shelf. Both the teacher's desk and the old bookshelf carried a pencil sharpener.

I looked around the room and absorbed the scene. I sighed deeply. To say I was unimpressed would be an understatement. If I were going to be in this room for three years, then this was no time to mourn my lamentable state.

"Well, this is certainly no state-of-the-art classroom. But I bet I can get it looking better as soon as they remove these junk from this room. There are too many chairs and this whole shelf, along with its content, has outlived its usefulness."

"Miss Wright, no, man, in here really look bad—I mean! Well, all the same—let me see the Spanish stuff. Maybe I can use some." Donna's second area of study is Spanish, so this room held treasures for her.

When I opened the door near the chalkboard that led to the little room, I realized that it had another door that connected to Tonetta's classroom. I didn't prolong my enquiry because an avalanche of books, boxes, folders, and other objects seemed to pose an imminent threat.

My work had just started. We had to make trips to the 300 building to collect the set texts for our classes, and then carry them back to our classrooms. We had to physically arrange the class furnishings. I thought of my former school where students were responsible for collecting their texts (except when there was one set and it was shared by other teachers). The custodians would clean and arrange the classrooms and teachers make adjustments for grouping. As I lugged books and other materials to my room, I missed Jamaica.

I heard that it was possible to get borders and papers from the office, so I went and got what I could. After that I made trips to Teachers' Shops and other stores in Greenville and Martin County in order to get teaching aids, motivational charts and other articles to lift the appearance, smell and general ambience. I cut my Jamaican calendars and pasted them on poster boards. Resorting to my computer and calligraphy skills, I created motivational charts with a cultural slant. I worked on my cultural corner with different Jamaican newspapers: *The Jamaica Observer, The Daily Gleaner, Youth Link, Children's Own* and calendars. I had brochures of the tourists' resorts, magazines from the national airline, map, charts, stamps, phone cards and other paraphernalia. I really went to town on this display!

There were some old computers in the little room and I found that they could work, so I asked for a cable and Tonetta and I made the connections. When some of the boxes toppled over, I saw an old printer. I plugged it in and connected it to the computer and, after a few slaps, it too worked. Yes, I was in business! At that time I had to use two students' desks pushed together for the computer and printer. After much effort, one of the custodians found an old table. It was salvaged from the stock destined for disposal. I gave Donna the extra desks and chairs leaving about twenty-eight for my class. I certainly hoped that the class would not be larger than that, because the room could not hold anymore desks comfortably.

I worked from morning until evening, trying to get that room ready. Opening night found me sitting in a presentable classroom. The Program had given us some useful materials at the orientation. I was especially grateful for the world map, and a little chart which welcomed visitors to the classroom of an international teacher. I labeled the door with my name, the subject and the class. I would later write this on a folder which formed a pocket for the bubble sheet, used to indicate the attendance each day.

My heart fluttered as I waited for my first parents and children to arrive. The evening was losing its color fast as the darkness advanced. I was startled when the phone rang. I saw that it was Donna.

"Hi, how are things over there?" I asked; glad to have someone other than myself to talk to.

"Some students just passed through. Boy, Miss. Wright, you wan' see dem!"

"I am still waiting to see some. One or two peeped in, but they were merely curious. Someone is coming. We'll talk later."

My first guests were a woman and her daughter. The girl was one of the four token whites in my first semester. I fought hard to hide my amusement as the girl squirmed. Her mother was very proud of her and was quite willing to talk about her and her sister. She was not going to miss this chance to talk about her pride and joy, even as the girl told her to stop and began to edge toward the door. I could understand both positions and turned up my enthusiasm a few volts to make both of them feel comfortable. We were saved by the appearance of two other women arriving.

I smiled warmly and greeted them.

"Evening, is you Ms. Wright?"

I was taken aback by the abruptness. It was not just the tone, but the look—oh that look! They looked at me as though I was some strange creature that they were about to buy against their better judgment. As they watched me, I was trying to figure out which one was the parent. I was keeping up a steady stream of information, merely stating the obvious. I asked for their names.

The one I thought was the parent spoke up. "Dat's ma frayend. I'm a comin' to your class."

I was learning fast. From that point on, I did not make any assumptions. I began to wonder if all the students would be so physically mature and, if so, what would be their attitude to work and authority. After that there were only six more students and parents in attendance. I was not sure what to think because my class list said I should have at least sixty students and having eight attending opening night was hardly a promise of something better to come.

At approximately eight-thirty, Tonetta knocked at the door. "Marjorie, they say we should come to the front of the building because it is getting dark and this is a bit far."

"So when did they find this out? Not only are we at the back of the school, but the main building is locked off from us. There is not even a fence to separate us from the outside. Well, well…"

I learned later that some parents didn't wish to come all the way to the back as they thought it was too far. It was for that reason I had seen so few of them. Since our cars were parked at the front, we packed up our things and left for the night. The first couple of lesson plans were written, since we have to teach rules and procedures at the outset.

CHAPTER NINE

Teaching or Crowd Control - What's the Teacher's Role?

Day 2 Wishes
Tuesday, 28, August, 2007

Good morning,

I know that yesterday was a long and exciting day for you!! As the culmination of your many weeks of preparation, I hope that it met your expectations...

Take a deep breath and think about all the experiences you have at your fingertips ... including your vast store of personal knowledge, as well as the many Program and district resources available to you. Use your best strategies and techniques to make your classroom an exciting source of knowledge for your students!

Please know that we have you in our thoughts this week ... Take one day at a time and remember that you have a three-day weekend ahead to regroup and prepare for the coming autumn weeks.

Hope your second day is both productive and enjoyable.

Teacher Support Specialist

The first day had come and gone. There were obvious cultural differences. Some of them were good indicators of some bad practices in the society and the school system. Sadly, many of the students were very interested in the dross of the Jamaican experience. The majority of them wanted to know things like:

"You all have weed in Jamaica? I mean ganja; I hear it's good there."

"Did you smoke weed in Jamaica? I bet you were high all the time!"

"Can you do the 'Dutty Wine'? You can dance?"

"Did you watch 'Shattas'? Dat was one bad mother %$#! My bad, my bad!"

"Are there prostitutes in Jamaica?"

"Why you come to Bertie? Bertie aint no place! I can't wait to get out of this place."

"Can you curse? You know, can you swear? Can you tell us some Jamaican bad words? We won't tell nobody! How come, Miss--- tell us then."

When I asked them to take home the letters to their parents and to have the form on the rules and guidelines for the school signed and returned, I must say the response took me by surprise.

"Is you going to give me a hundred?"

"A hundred what, for what?"

"A hundred marks and a 'A', for returning it!"

"Are you serious?" They were as bright as hundred-watt bulbs. How could they ask such a thing?

"Yeah, you don't know that?" they asked looking at me, as if they really could not believe that I didn't know that. "We gotta get a hundred if we take it back." What an incentive! At that rate they wouldn't have to be able to read to pass through the system!

This news was shocking to me, but they were not done. Later I discovered that they were very helpful to each other in that a few students would do the work and then the others would reproduce it. They had no problems with it. In Jamaica, it was common for students to cover their work from roving eyes and a few would share. The majority of students were competitive, so they hoped to get that edge by not sharing. While I was aware of cheating at home, this was at a higher scale. They begged for worksheets and lambasted any attempt on my part to teach. They were most vocal about my attempts to encourage them to think and write, which is what I was employed to do.

"Why do you ask so much questions—dang!"

"These topics are whack! All you ever give us is boring trash. Who can write about that crap?"

"Keep in mind, school is not meant to be entertaining. If you get some in the process enjoy it, but your objective in school is to learn." I reminded them.

These topics actually came from the list of past tests given by the State. I had received a set from the County office. Once I had established that the students could write legibly and that they understood the concept of a complete sentence, I set about teaching them to build paragraphs with details. To develop their ability to provide details, I used comic strips and cartoons from the newspapers. I especially liked the comic strips, like "Henry," that related an account without the use of words. The students were then guided to develop the story by careful words selection to create details and a vivid picture of what was happening. This activity was meant to teach them the power of observation which is a valuable skill for essay writing. It took a lot of patience, but they were pleased with the final product. Because I was working with each child, taking each one through the writing process, the act of cheating was severely curtailed. It was hard work because these students did not like to write. They hated the process, but for those who persisted and went from planning, drafting with the sequence map, writing and editing to publishing, they were richly rewarded.

As teachers, we were provided a Pacing Guide. This guide set out the literature, themes and skills to be developed in accord with the goal and objective of the state and county. The list to be covered over the semester was staggering when you take into account the students' competency level and other factors that were adversely affecting the teaching learning process. I never lost sight of the fact that my main objective was to get the students ready for the State Writing Test in March. There was one cause for consolation. I found out that the writing test was merely one essay to be done in three hours. I could not believe it! Perhaps our children in the Caribbean will soon charge us with child abuse. They have two-and-a-half hours to answer two short-answer response comprehensions from different genre, an advertisement, letter to the editor, poem, drama, etc. They must write a summary or report, a narrative of three hundred to four-hundred-and-fifty words, and a persuasive piece in about two-hundred-and-fifty words—all in one sitting! For years I had successfully taught students to do this in the allotted time. Perhaps these students were so easily distracted because so little was expected of them. How can one rise to such low expectations or rise to high expectation so suddenly?

When they became frustrated—and it didn't take much to frustrate them—they would turn on me. They tried many things and said even more. One boy, whom I still think can have a good life and excel, was often absent from school. He was either in jail or the courthouse. I felt pity for him.

One day after a disagreement he said, "I think the teacher is a supercilious ass!"

I asked him to repeat what he said, a technique I use to get people to retract and review questionable statements. They often do not repeat and I usually take it as a small consolation.

"Miss Wright, I said asinine." He was being rude and had his foot in his mouth. I was especially aware of his use of words.

I decided not to take offence, but to use the opportunity to show him and the class the power of words. This was the SAT class where each week they were given a list of words to learn. He was learning; he only needed to be taught to use words for good. I took him aside and reprimanded him. The next day he came to class with a severe cut on his hand.

"Miss Wright, I have something to say, seriously. When I got this cut, I had an epiphany and…" he proceeded to tell me how he was seeing things differently and he was going to lead a different life from that point on.

Not all my attempts to teach turned out to be like that. Some of my slowest students were in that semester. I remember one day I was really trying to keep them on task. There was a boy sitting in the front with a photo album. There were about four students that were more interested in those pictures than in what I was trying to do. I spoke to them about it and the next thing I knew they were all poring over it studiously again. I tell you—something in me snapped. I marched over there, snatched that album and threw it in the bin.

The class was stunned. Then they began to close their mouths and breathe again. One-by-one they started to relate to each other what they just witnessed.

"Miss Wright, you is crazy!" they declared vehemently.

"She be trippin!"

The boy came up to me. He was breathing short and his lips and hands were trembling.

"What'd you do that for?" he asked quietly.

"How many times did I ask you to put it away?" I was looking at his face and was ready to do battle. I was tired of the foolishness!

"You threw my thing in the trash!" He hissed, then turned and walked to the small table beneath the telephone and picked up the eighteen SAT texts and dropped them in the trash can. All this seemed to take place in slow motion. I stood and watched and I laughed. I suppose I was crazy. He walked out the door and I continued my class. Everybody was quiet and attentive, except for an occasional, "Man, she be crazy!"

I heard strong, purposeful steps striding up the board ramp. Mr. Early, one of the principals, darkened the doorway. He called me and asked what had happened. I explained and he told me to be careful. I should not take students' property and throw it in the trash. He went and took the books from the trash can. I don't know what, if anything was said to the boy. While he was removing the books from the trash and cleaning them (another student had gone over and thrown the rest of his drink in the trash can), another principal, Mrs. Sanderson arrived. She sympathized with me and asked me to try and keep it together. I promised to try, but remarked on how indifferent the students were and the difficulty I was having trying to keep them interested in the lessons.

As we stood on the porch, I felt like crying out of sheer frustration. I looked on the main school building and thoughts of the Virginia Tech massacre flashed before me. Were these students really worth my life?

I prepared the first progress report and issued them. For the first time there was a flurry of interest among the students. There was one boy that I don't think I will ever forget. He was fine looking with beautiful skin and teeth. He was the last to arrive and the first to depart the classroom. On the rare occasion that he was present, he reeked of cigarette smoke. Other than cigarettes, the only other thing I saw him with was a hair brush. Yet he was a very active student. Here is the extent of his activities: he slept, passed gas, or lay on two chairs where he would thrust upwards and groan erotically. I had reported him to the office, Guidance, asked other teachers what to do about him and then I appealed to Mr. Early. He laughed and said that the boy had been at the school for as long as he had been there and that he did not know what else to do about him.

When the boy received his report, he looked at it, Test—0; Group Work—0; Class Work/Homework—0; Absence—9.

"Hey, Miss Wright, this ain't right!"

"What's not right?"

"This not right, you give me 9 absences. It should be 10."

"OK, I'll be sure to correct that for you sir."

When I went to the workshop and professional development put on by the Program that fall, I was asked by the Teacher Support Specialist how I was getting on.

"I heard that you have been having some challenges."

Now who told her that and forgot to tell me that they had noticed? I related to her the above experience. I had gone on to have other discussions with the student. He was twenty years old, in grade ten and was still not sure what he would do with his life. When I pressed him, he said he liked mechanics and would like to become a truck driver.

"What else can you do if that fails?" I watched the toothpick in his mouth move from one corner to the next.

He ran his hand over the waves in his hair then said, "I guess I could work as a laborer."

"But what would you labor at?"

He thought for awhile. "At the slaughter house, you know where they kill pigs and chickens."

"Do you know that, if you learn a skill, you can go to Canada to work? I heard that they need workers and that you can earn a thousand dollars per week there."

"How would I get there? I don't have money."

"First, you must get the skill. That's what I did and see me here now. If you got the skill, I would see that you get the money to go there."

He laughed when I told him this. This is the second student to laugh at me when I offered to help.

When I related the account to the lady she said, "You would be surprised, but, you know some truck drivers are better paid than teachers!" I looked at her and she turned a little red in the face and her blue gray eyes shifted from mine.

Hearing that made me think seriously about what Asante Moran, a teacher, had said to Barack Obama about the public school system: "The public school system is not about educating black children. Never has been. Inner-city schools are about social control, period."

One British head teacher, with whom I had an interview, called it "crowd control", and a CNN reporter described it as "controlled chaos." Everybody is aware that the system is sick, but nobody seems to care enough to agitate for it to be well. Teachers are made the scapegoat of the society.

The main principal, Mrs. Burns, had stopped by the classroom a few times unofficially. It was a curious thing that she never initiated any feedback—good, bad or indifferent. I took it upon myself to visit with her and to describe the problems I was having, which I am sure she was privy to, as she sometimes saw us in the library. She gave me some insight into the effect of the drug culture on this generation. I learned that some of the students really had severe mental and emotional problems which had significantly affected their mental state.

"I must confess that when I envisioned coming to the US, I didn't foresee this level of backwardness."

"I understand what you mean. There are parts of the States that are not yet in the twenty-first century."

"Perhaps the educators can do more. Unless the parents are taught to expect more from the system and push their children to do better the cycle is just going to continue."

"How would you suggest they do this?"

"Well, I noticed that parents who appear to express an interest in their children are mainly interested in a pass. They seem unconcerned about the process to get it. One parent was surprised to learn that her daughter was taking SAT. I wanted to get her help to get the girl focused. She said her daughter was not going to college. When I explained to her the importance of a skill or a college education, she seemed genuinely surprised. After the effort of the community leaders to get us here, I think they should've tried to get the community on board—make them understand or see their mission."

"You have a point. Perhaps you can write about this."

"You're right. I am sure of one thing. What I have been engaged in since I've been here is not teaching. I can count the few times I managed to really teach anything. They seem to be hooked on worksheets. I don't get the concept of make-up work. When a student misses a class, how can some worksheet make up for the absence, when they have missed what was taught? Based on what I have been seeing, the teacher is redundant."

"Well, next Semester you won't have the same group and I think you won't have the SAT students, so it should be different."

"I hope so. I really hope that is the case."

Donna was moved to the Spanish Department and I have yet to see someone as happy as she was. Her class was in the main building near the office and her students were different from mine. Some were even said to be on the honor roll. Her students' parents were actually interested. Donna had become frustrated with the demands for grade, the quarrels over getting an "A" and the demands of planning and correcting students' work. Now that she was in the Spanish Department, she would not be in the main building, but her students would be those who opt to do the course.

While all this was going on, we had to get our physical done, as well as our drivers' licenses. We studied and discussed the road signs and directions. Megan had lived and driven in the States before and she had gotten directions from Janice's husband. She showed me how to make the three-point turn and took me along the practice road. I then showed Donna. My experience at the DMV is worth telling, but I'll leave that for another time.

I don't think that my stay in North Carolina would have been complete without a visit to Vance County. To make this a reality, for the Thanksgiving break, I called my friend Marie. You remember Marie who seemed accident prone and who had invited me to visit her because of her fear of driving? That's the one. I invited Donna along, since she should have gone there as well. We needed closure. It was important to us to see what might have been. I received directions, copied a map from MapQuest, packed my air bed, blanket and a pillow and we set out. We made a few wrong turns from the map, but it was a pleasant ride. We saw such beauty in the natural landscape that we didn't mind losing our way. We even paused, like tourists, to take pictures of the trees, ablaze in their brilliant colors. I grew to love God the Artist, even more. Sometimes I just stopped so we could gaze at them—such beauty!

Marie had to come and get us because her direction from the town to her house was not graphic enough. We kept passing the turn somehow. Oh yes, she was driving. I think she forgot she was with us as she floored that pedal. I called her on the phone and reminded her that we were following. When I didn't see where she went, I simply stopped and waited for her to call. We eventually got to her flat—accident free!

The next evening she took us to her school and we were able to see a few classrooms because some men were painting and carrying out some general maintenance. We were particularly taken by a Science classroom she told us belonged to a young Philippine man. I think I would have been afraid to be in that classroom. Everything was so very neat; I couldn't imagine how they functioned with such perfection. I am not disorganized or am I untidy by any means, but I think that even Adrian Monk would have squirmed a bit in that room. Miss Luisa would be a distant second if they were competing. Marie was giving us the grand tour. We passed a big tree with the brightest, most luxurious yellow foliage you ever saw. It went down in our cameras' memories as well as ours.

"Let me show you where they wait on the bus a evening time when school let off." We walked to the area.

"But a so it look like where they keep animals?" I didn't know what else to think. There were chains and metal bars that created several passages, like those I would see on cattle farms in Jamaica.

"Me say, you want to see how dem run in the bus when the teachers pull dem chain a evening time! When I see them the first time I couldn't believe it. Then Margery, a same so dem run like a cow, you know!" She still seemed to be coming to terms with it even though she was in her second year.

"Marie, you tink they behave like animals because they treat dem like animals?"

"Boy, me no know—you know, but dem a something else."

"A true you know, well, a mean, Miss Wright, look at our school. Well, you remember, we have to take them to the lunch room—a mean, you know… den we have to sit with them and watch them. Then in the evening, well we have to have people at the bus again, gee—people have to make sure they go on the bus and – you know, dem not babies." Donna was really trying to fathom what was behind it all. She had made a valid observation and I concurred.

"I suspect you're right. They really seem wild; they seem to be uncomfortable with themselves and intolerant of adults. So Marie, how do you find them at the Middle School?"

"Me dear, the other day I had to lean a little one in a corner an say, 'Look on me! You see dat me bigger dan you? Look on me good and listen when me talk to you!' Me say you wan' see that little brute shake. A so you have to do them. They not used to nice treatment." I am five-feet-seven and I have always had to look up to Marie, so I could only imagine that encounter.

That night we went to dinner with some other teachers who were also on the program. There were some from Virginia and others from other counties in NC. That night was like a therapy session. Everybody had some interesting stories to tell. We talked, ate and laughed. For the whole time we shared stories of delinquent children and their attitude to authority. When we got home, Marie started another chapter; this was her own experience in the first year.

"Margery me a tell you, you know man, last year every evening me come home and bawl. Dem pickney get on with some tings. Then because I wasn't used to the system they got away with murder! Me cry before me go a school and me cry when me come home."

"Marie, you know, sometimes I think that I've put off crying for too long."

"Me did bawl bredda!"

"Now I am angry and I know I'm crying deep down inside, but the tears just won't come. You know when you watch movies and you see people crying an' a dem nose dem a wipe? A dat a happen to me."

"Well, this year I ready fi dem!"

"I don't think I want another year of this. This is not teaching, man! Some of the teachers tell me that some other schools are better."

"Yes, it's true, but it is hard to get into them."

"And, from what I've heard, the agency is not very helpful with reassigning teachers to other schools. I'm leaving; I can't endure another year like this. I really don't need to do this."

"So, did you tell them?"

"I spoke with the principal. You know that at the Fall Workshop, they said something to the effect that, if you go home before completing the Program you may be considered a failure? I would love them to endure my experience and see if they would still feel the same way. I wanted to do the Masters, but I can't see it happening with the work load and demands I have to meet."

"I plan to start, you know. I have the entry exam next week."

"That's very good and I wish you all the best. You know what happened to me? At the workshop, I told Dr. T about some of the problems I was having. Other members of the group also listed the problems and we proceeded to make solutions. He sent me some good suggestions. I started right away to put some in place. One that was really working was to write, "Bathroom Pass" on a big card board so as to discourage them from asking to go out so often. Next thing I knew, there is an announcement that we can only use hall passes that the school issues."

"That's how they are, me dear. It's as if they working against you instead of with you. If it works and nobody gets hurt, they should just let it stay."

"Well, I decide that I don't need this. If I needed the money, perhaps I would suffer it a little, but that's not the case. I can't see any reason to justify this suffering anymore."

Later, that big bathroom sign had to be thrown out because a used condom was found sticking on it. I had suspected for some time that my classroom was being used for sexual trysts. To my great consternation, I found out that my desk was providing the base. It was not comfortable to sit there anymore. They stole the chocolate I kept in the cabinet to use as incentive and they stole students' work from the cabinet and used them to complete their own assignments.

We were glad to have visited with Marie in Vance, but concluded that I preferred my living accommodations in Williamston. After all, I had central heating and air condition with our own washer and drier. It was also clear that the social problems persisted there, so we would have been subjected to similar oppression. We left Marie with her promise to return the visit.

We went to Virginia Beach to shop for winter clothes. Although I traveled with Donna and her heart throb, Megan and I shared a hotel room. I woke up every time a toilet was flushed in the hotel. Those toilets could really use some silencers. We were up and ready for shopping early the next day. It was one of those days that ended badly. Several times when we traveled together in separate cars, there were some near misses. More often than not, the leading car driver was moving without much thought for the others. Since we were a group of about four cars, we should have been driving at a moderate speed and slowing after traffic lights, if all didn't make it through. Because of this negligence, the driver at the back often had difficulty keeping pace and sometimes took dangerous risks in an effort to keep up. In this case, they were not able to escape all of the risks. The last car was totaled in a collision with an SUV at the traffic light and we spent the rest of the day at the hospital. They were not seriously injured, but the incident pulled a wet blanket over the day. We got home late that night.

I had not bought much, but I was not too concerned. I had a relatively good buy of a coat that was good for cold or rain. Knowing that Erica, my sister in New York, was sending my blanket and some tops, I focused on getting thermal under clothes. We were advised to "pad up" for the winter. Since most of my clothes were modest fits from England, they would still do if I wore the thermals underneath. Between a sister at the Kingdom

Hall and my housemate, I had three coats and I decided that those should be enough to see me through the winter.

There were not many opportunities to feel cold. I was always in the car or in a building. It was usually a short walk from one point to the next. I did not bother to park all the way to the front of the school. The pine trees at the back provided enough cover for the car. It was only when I went preaching door to door, that I had continual exposure to the elements or at school when I had to go to the 100 or 300 buildings to use the toilets.

It was a different matter in the classroom. The students would come and without even a greeting, they would bark, "Turn de heat on!" or "Turn de heat off!" This was a cause for many disputes among them as some were cold and the others were hot. And everybody wanted their needs met without any sacrifice on their part.

My well-deserved December break was spent in New York. Marilyn took me to Rocky Mount to get the Amtrak train and it was, "New York, here I come!" When I got to Penn Station, Erica and her friend, Pat, found me after several call and responses. When we got home, it was early the next morning. The journey from NC to NY by train was longer than traveling from London to NY by plane. I was just too happy to be away from school to mind the distance. When the train moved away from NC so did my thoughts from my situation.

The first time I saw snow, was on this trip to New York. If I had seen it falling, nobody would have had a laugh at my ignorance. We were visiting Daddy in the Bronx when I saw some frosty ice on the ground. It was in a pile. I thought it was odd that someone should clean their freezer and just leave the ice in the garden like that. It was only a small amount. Erica commented on how cold it was and said something about the snow. I was wondering, where was the snow she was talking about?

On our way back, we were driving past a McDonald's restaurant when I noticed a huge mound of whitish grey in the parking lot against the fence. I could not help, but asking, "Why they have that plastic looking thing in the parking lot?"

"Where?" Erica asked. I indicated the area and she burst out laughing. "You no see dat a snow!" How was I to know?

There was slush one rainy night, but still no sight of snow falling. It was not until I was back in NC that I had my first experience of falling snow. Marilyn and I went outside and pranced around in it and giggled gleefully. It was not a lot, but the flakes were large and floating lightly like dandelion seeds or cotton in a gentle breeze. The simple pleasure made my heart melt too. It felt so good to be able to let go, forget work and enjoy that moment.

The much-anticipated end of the first semester was not just looming any longer, it had come. I was glad it did. The second semester would be very busy for obvious reasons. It would be the semester for workshops, State Writing Tests, more benchmark tests, and the inevitable evaluations.

The preparations for the Writing Test would be one of the events that drew me closer to Mrs. Williamston, the department chairperson. She was a passionate, no-nonsense woman. I grew to treasure our relationship although in my mind I thought of her as a fruit in Jamaica called June plum. The same fruit in the Eastern Caribbean is called golden apple. I love this fruit. When it is good and ripe, the skin may be a little tangy, but the inside is juicy and refreshing. However, if you bite too deeply in the fruit, you may be pricked by the seed which has small spikes and is quite prickly. If you are patient and careful, you can enjoy even the seed of this fruit. We would sit and chat and she would tell me stories about her family. Soon I felt as if I knew her feisty mother, her siblings, her daughters and adoring husband. I admired her love of teaching and her desire to improve the young people that she was privileged to have in her charge.

She was the designated driver when we had to attend a Saturday workshop for the Test-Ready Session. On that journey I got an insight in the culture of the school and the community at another level. She was a very good story teller and had a mannerism that reminded me of Reba McIntyre. I was very careful in my dealings with her, so as not to incur her displeasure. This did not mean that we always agreed, but our healthy respect for each other allowed us to listen and acknowledge the facts of whatever issues we were discussing. There were those occasions too when I made every effort to apply the simple advice I was given: smile and nod.

This was a crucial bit of caution because, in general, many of the people were related or were quite close in their friendships. You may not be aware of those relationships and, therefore, you did not want to speak ill of any one and have it come back to haunt you. It has always been my policy to not say anything behind someone that I would not be willing to say to their face. This has saved my skin many times.

There was one case at my old school where we had some slackers in the Industrial Arts Department. One of the very outspoken senior teachers was very upset because many of us form teachers were being prevented from completing our reports, by Mr. Raymond. He was notorious for his slothful demeanor.

She began to rant, "That man is so damn lazy, you wouldn't believe it! All he does is stands and stares through the windows. Even the children know him. Do you know that they say he doesn't teach them a thing? He just looks out the window and ask them for baby names! I have never come across another teacher so lazy. He doesn't teach. He doesn't even mark the exam papers!" She was fuming as she called out the list of faults against him. I knew what she meant and I had had my own experiences and evidence of his indolence.

I decided to add fuel to the fire she had started. "You remember when I was collecting the students' attendance record for grade ten? I noticed that every day he had the same figures, rain or shine. I asked him how was it possible to have the same figures every morning, since sometimes some students are late or absent. He asked me if he should change them up sometimes. I explained that if he would arrive early and go to the classroom like the rest of us, the figures would fluctuate automatically and he wouldn't need to make them up."

"You see that? Me no tell you man—damn lazy! Did you know that he produced final exam grades for students who have not attended school since the beginning of the term?"

For some strange reason I looked up at that point and there was Mr. Raymond, just turning away from staring out the staffroom window. He was behind us all that time. He must have heard everything.

I turned the conversation over to him. "Mr. Raymond, you must agree that it look bad that way... How you explain it?"

He asked what I meant. The senior teacher seemed to have swallowed her tongue. We were interrupted and he moved on. I was glad to see that the senior teacher had not suffered anything serious from the shock.

"Laad Jesus, Margery, you did know say him behind we all along?" she asked.

"No. But we weren't telling any lies on him. Even he agrees that it was odd. When you speak the truth and intend no harm by it, you shouldn't feel guilty. Somebody needs to tell him the truth—nicely, of course."

Every school has its slackers and NC is no exception. I met the female version of Mr. Raymond while I was there. I was given a list of teachers who had a non-contact period or Planning Session during the Fourth Block. I needed to take off the following afternoon because I had an appointment. Everybody that I knew well enough to ask had already made plans since it was a Friday afternoon. As a last resort, I decided to ask a teacher who was a native, but she was on the quiet and simple side. I had overheard the students speaking about her and knew that they held her in very low regard. They said that Mr. Early was planning to sever her employment at the school. Because of their temperament, I did not think it was kind to ask her, but I was desperate.

I knocked on her door and opened it. As my eyes became adjusted to the dim, I saw her resettling in her skin. "Oh, Ms. Wright, you frightened me!"

"I'm sorry, but I knocked."

"Yes I heard the knock, but when you entered, I thought you were from county office because you look so—business-like and formal, dressed like that and here I'm cutting out."

"Cutting out?" I was not familiar with the expression.

"You know, not teaching, I thought they had dropped in unannounced and found me not teaching."

She was sitting staring out the window and the children were minding their own business, reading, talking on the phone—which is not allowed, listening to iPods and MP3 players, also forbidden, playing electronic games—all illegal. Little wonder the students thought I was tripping, when I tried to keep them occupied for the period. Somebody had already asked her to sit in so she suggested another teacher down the hall. When I went to that teacher she agreed, but said no, when she heard where the classroom was located. When I started to complain about how difficult it was to find someone, she suggested that I take the work to her and leave instruction that the students should come to her room instead. However, she was absent the following day, so I had to start my search all over with time running out.

I merely wanted a cover for half-the-block because one of the Art teachers had offered to do the first half. I eventually found someone willing. He was a young white male teacher. He was quiet, mild tempered and willing. You would think you could still see the mother's milk on his face. Talk about leaving the lamb to guard the wolves! I felt bad, but time was running out and I could not find anybody else who was willing. I had to catch the train in Rocky Mount to travel to New York to make my appointment in New Jersey on Saturday.

When I returned to school, I saw some acronyms for the writing process written on the chalkboard in strong, confident strokes. Somehow I could not associate the writing with Mr. Phillips, the young teacher whom I had asked to sit in for me. When I asked the students about it, there was a commotion. I asked them to be quiet so that I could hear what was being said.

Devaun, a high-strung, ball of energy was begging to speak. "I'm a tell you how it went down—a'ight. 't was that woman—a'ight—you know the one—she tink she betta than us—yea. I jus cuss her out!"

"Woo-woo, just a minute now, you are talking about a teacher here! Did you just say, you 'cuss her out'? What do you mean by that?"

He stood, licked his lips like Maurice Greene, lifted his polo shirt and rubbed his stomach. He did his laugh which was a cross between the sound made by ram goat and a cat sneeze. All eyes were on him and he was reveling in the attention. I decided that I did not wish to hear what had happened in that atmosphere.

I decided to set them straight. "From what I'm hearing, things didn't go well during my absence on Friday. I am disappointed that you could not have used the opportunity to learn something worthwhile from one of the best teachers in the system. I have been listening to you all—and Jeovani, I have not forgotten that you said, 'I don't have to listen to you, you is just a Jamaican teacher'. This incident on Friday tells me you don't want to listen to an American teacher either! She has been in the system for over twenty years and you want to tell me, she has nothing to teach you?

"Look around you… you see that old computer with a printer that I have to slap to get it to work sometimes? Do you see the cracks in the floor? This," I indicated the structure, "this is a mobile unit that is falling apart as we speak. We are trying our best here!"

"Yeah, they don't respect us, they not giving us proper resources." They were beginning to speak up.

I did not wish to hear them at that time. "And I don't blame them if this is how you show your appreciation for quality teachers. What reason is there for them to believe that you would show any more appreciation for better facilities? Just up the road they are building a state-of-the-art prison. Now keep in mind—I am a foreigner, invited here to teach. Who do you think they plan to put in that prison? I hope you see what is happening. This system is designed to produce inmates. If you want to be among them, you don't have to come here and make other people's lives miserable."

I was not pleased. When I saw Mrs. Williamston, she explained what had happened. She is the buddy teacher for Mr. Phillips. It was while she was visiting him during his planning that she learned of our arrangement. She encouraged him to use the time to plan and volunteered to go to my class instead.

She said, "Darling, my heart goes out to you—um hum! Is that really what you've had to deal with all this time? And that little __ Devaun, is going to tell me about—'when you all was back in slavery…!' He's so dumb, he doesn't even know that I wasn't around during slavery. I tell you, those little __ __ carried on… I didn't even get a chance to teach a thing!"

I was grinning from ear-to-ear. I felt sorry for her, but now more than ever, I was convinced that I was not the problem. I felt reassured and exonerated.

"Mrs. Williamston, I'm sorry for what happened, but I am glad you had a chance to see what I'm up against every day. You think they were bad? You should see or hear my second block. There is a girl in there who gloats about their bad behavior. What I can't understand is why they place so many of the poor performers in the same group and with the same teacher!"

"That's the problem—it's that Ava Snow. She's the one who does the placements. I went straight around to the office and I told Mrs. Burns that it was not right…"

Never underestimate the power of having some locals in your corner. I had done relatively well in that area. I had one on lunch duty with me. She was a social worker and so we talked about some of my problem students. We covered for each other sometimes and she was able to help me with two of my major problem students in the first and second blocks.

There was Coach Ray Major. If Mrs. Williamston was a June Plum, then he was a cool jelly coconut on a hot day. He would help me with my fourth block and helped the Jamaican teachers to master the report system. Fourth block is the class of mainly problem boys. I even had an understanding with him in the latter part of the semester that I would send disruptive students to his room for time out. He was a blessing to us, Jamaican teachers, when it came to making our reports at the end of the semesters. He was respected by the students and I thought he provided what those boys needed, a father figure.

I had stopped writing referrals except for severe cases. I got to know who the students respected and got them to help me with the disciplining and correcting process. Since those who should render assistance were shirking their responsibilities, I would leave them be. When I forged ahead at times in order to complete topics and to try to keep up with deadlines, I would be so stressed I concluded that any success was merely a pyrrhic victory.

CHAPTER TEN

Sex, Rap and Review in the Classroom

"Yes, it's the truth I'm telling you. Margery, the little boy searches the garbage bin and takes out any bits of food he finds and eats it! He also steals from other students. I don't know what else to do with him."

"So have you been in touch with his parents?" Angela was telling me about her daily trials. It was one of our rituals, each week we would call and vent.

"My dear, I have spoken to the grandmother, but it is more than meets the eye. Apparently, the mother doesn't take very good care of him. When you see his skin it is ashy and he has this green mucus coming from his nose which he keeps licking. If he is not medicated, he acts up in class and becomes very disruptive. But the grandmother doesn't like when he is medicated because of the side effects."

"At least there are two of you in the room." I was referring to the other teacher who was assigned to work with her in the classroom. I often wish I had an assistant for the sake of the EC students.

"That's true, but that doesn't stop him from taking up my time. The other day he attacked, I thought he would punch me in my stomach. The principal caned him and to think that he was just coming back from suspension."

"What do you mean by suspension? These are what—six/seven year olds? Little wonder they are like gangrene in the society's foot by the time they get to the high school stage. I tell you, if nothing else, this place has provided me with some graphic metaphors. I was telling the principal of the STEM school the other day that I feel like I am a band-aid on gangrene in this school. Have you ever seen anything like this, Angela?"

"My dear, at least our principal don't joke with them, you know! She is very serious and she really supports us."

"Well, I am happy for you. You hear them say, 'Too many rats never dig a good hole'? I think that is the case here. I don't get the impression that they are working as a unit. You remember that incident I was telling you about with the boy who was practically sexually harassing me? The one I had to push off me?"

"Tell me again—what happened?"

"He had done it before and I warned him not to try it again. I was standing at the door to welcome them as usual. Their bell work was in place. Several boys had arrived, some greeted me and I greeted all. They went in—no problem. He arrived and, as usual, pretended to trip and to stumble into me. I pushed him off me and he smiled. I grabbed his sleeve and told him that was it and reminded him of the other times. He said, 'Get the #@% off me, bitch!'"

"Jesus—every time I hear it, it shocks me all over."

"I wrote him up, because that is a zero-tolerance offence. He went to Mr. Ocheato and he gave him three days In School Suspension. So I had to be doing extra work for that boy to get make-up work. Another boy told his friend that a teacher must be 'mad as hell...' and another principal gave him five days Out of School Suspension."

"Can you imagine that?"

"It got worse. When he returned from ISS, he threw down his release form on the podium and said, 'Yo, sign that!' I told him to take it and get out of my face. He said, 'You have to sign it!' So I said, 'Really now?' He went back to his seat after looking me up-and-down as though he would like to do me bodily harm and told his friends. They all started to tell me about the law and what I had to do. I told them to sue me and he walked out. Shortly after, the receptionist called me to find out why I refused to sign the form. When I explained she said, 'Write him up. That is disrespectful.'

"At the end of the block, I went to the office. The boy was with Mrs. Sanderson. She asked me what happened and I told her. She said, 'But that should have been an out-of-school suspension.' The boy had told her that I had 'mushed' his face. She said, 'I know that's a lie—Ms. Wright—no way!' I asked her what 'mush' was and she demonstrated it for me. It was the act of placing the open hand or fingers on the face and pushing it back forcefully. I had to laugh. Me? I had never done that to anybody in my life, not even with affection. We talked and he apologized. I called his home and encouraged them to urge him to be more conscious and productive in class."

"Well, Margery, you really have it to deal with at your school. At least these are small. What hurts even more is how they love to talk about their rights, but they don't remember that you and the other students have rights too."

"That's the problem. Have you written your plans already?"

"I have a few to go before I submit them. I don't know what time I'll finish tonight."

"See, we get to school with the sun, leave when it is leaving and then work most of the night. Then they want to tell me that this is not neo-slavery?"

"You're right you know, girl, this is really slavery—you're so right."

"What can I say, that's my name."

"What? Oh, you go on, Miss Wright." We both laughed and ended on that light note.

It was bantering like that that kept us going. The need to be able to talk things through cannot be overstated. I kept telling myself that I did not intend to go to prison or court for any of those children, so I learned to absorb the shock and abuse.

Now when I say shocks, I mean shocks! There was a boy in first semester, whose first and last names are informal names for the penis.

Usually, he would sit to the front of the class, but, this day in particular he was sitting to the back of the class. I had given instructions and was moving around to supervise their work. I noticed that he seemed dazed as he sat with his right elbow on the desk and his hand stroking his hair absentmindedly. The left hand was beneath the desk. It is my style to go up to students quietly to monitor their work or just to stand near them as a reminder to keep on task.

At first, I thought he was playing with a baseball bat, but this was only possible if it was turned upside down and the handle was in his pants leg. It took awhile for me to realize what was going on. I thought I would've died from consternation. I didn't say anything to him – what could I have said?

Somehow, he got my mark book and added some grades and improved others. Naturally, he failed first semester. I was appalled to see him in my class again for the second semester. He had grown a little and so had his pride in his "baseball bat." He was so proud of it that he got it ready for games one day in class. He swung it at the others and he drew up the waist of his pants so that they could see its impression.

I tried to give him a strike out when I said, "Has everybody seen it? Okay, sit down now and stop using my class for advertising anything else. I'm sure you don't want a third semester in English Two." They laughed at him. He sat down and we went back to work. Sometimes making light of a situation defuses the atmosphere without any lasting harm.

Sex was never far away from their minds. It was not just sex, but there was a degree of depravity with which I did not want to become accustomed. For example, one day a boy raced into the classroom and stood beside his chair with both hands holding the desk. He was bending over the desk and was pretending to be catching his breath, so he was panting dramatically. Another boy ran in, stood behind him and began to simulate sodomy. The rest of the class joined in by cheering them on.

Later on in the semester, the boy who was behind had to be sent home because he claimed responsibility for sticking the word "DICK" on my back. By this time, I did not need any further reason to resign, but there would be many more.

The beginning of the second semester was especially crucial because those new students had to be ready for the test in the first week of March. I chose to put aside the online school and to focus on the task at hand. We had a class set of the text North Carolina Writing Coach. This text was good to use to teach the form of writing in a limited time. I had to take them through the different exercises. The book provided some good working examples of effective writing techniques. We read the different sample essays in order to model the skills displayed.

A reader was assigned to read a problem/solution essay on teenage pregnancy. Her voice had just faded on the last word when the silence was shattered.

"DAT'S A DAMN LIE!"

When we recovered from the shock of the vehemence from a girl in the middle of the room, I ventured tentatively—these students are like bombs, you never know what may cause them to explode. "What is a lie?" I enquired.

"Dem family class don' stop no pregnancy. All dem kids dat go, is dem dat be pregnant."

"Now dat's a damn lie," a boy responded. "I went and I didn't get pregnant." The class was uproarious. I decided to try again,

"Did you attend the class?"

"Yea?"

"But you're not pregnant," she cut me off.

"Cause my mama done tell me wha' to do. You got kids, Miss Wright?" she asked me.

Another student piped up, "Nope, she not married and she's a Jehovah's Witness."

She tried again, "So you have a boyfriend?"

I was beaten to the response again,

"No, fool, she be a Christian!" At least this one was listening at the beginning of the term when all these personal details were discussed.

"So that mean you not having sex! Dang! I'm a work with you, Miss Wright—from now on I'm a work with you!"

I had a laugh at this. She made it seem as though it explained everything to her. Later outside of class, she saw me and picked up where she'd left off. "Ooh, Miss Wright, you don't know how I love that thing the boys have—ummhum" and she closed her eyes and smiled blissfully.

I tried to tell her that I understood it was designed to be pleasurable, but that it should be enjoyed in the context that God intended. I yearned to help her, but there was always someone to remind you that you can't quote the Bible to them. I had never seen a greater need for the healing effect of God's word or the degenerating effect because of a lack of it.

The sex madness was not only with the students. Several evenings I would be in the classroom writing my plans, preparing the board for next day, catching up on emails or correcting papers, when one of the custodians who swept the room, would just open the door suddenly. He would look at me, walk in the room, checked the small room then left. At first he would apologize for frightening me, and then he'd stopped pretending. He would just come, open the door swiftly, look in suspiciously, grin with what was left of his teeth, then leave.

"All things are clean to clean people."

It was not until Mrs. Williamston told me of the obscenities that went on in the classrooms, even among teachers, that I understood what they were trying to get at. I should have thought of it since I had seen evidence of it in the past.

Interestingly, I could have been among those statistics too. Had it not been for my Bible-trained conscience, I could have added some valuable fuel to the local gossip machine. If you think that I could have been in a setting like that and not have some sexual issues of my own to deal with, then you are more naïve than I was at the time.

By now you know that I treasure the Bible. Not only because it is inspired by God, but also because of the candor with which the men had written it. As I relate my own experience, I am mindful of that and will attempt to convey this sensitive experience with due diligence.

Many evenings we would go home, my housemate and I, and we were exhausted. That word will have to do because of my inability to find more graphic terms to describe how tired we were. It was especially true on Friday evenings. Marilyn could not understand why I would still be doing school work. If I didn't do it then, I would have to do it Saturday or Sunday and I was really endeavoring to keep those days free for spiritual activities.

She would say, "Girl, put down the old paper dem. Make we watch TV and enjoy we weekend of good-for-nothingness!"

"If I don't do them now, I'll have to do them later. I may as well watch and mark. Tomorrow I have service." She would sometimes get a set of papers and we would eat pizza, watch TV, grade papers, chat and laugh. The following afternoon when I returned from door-to-door work, I would then have my period of good-for-nothingness.

It was on those Friday afternoons that I would tell Marilyn, "You know, it is times like now that I'm sorry that I'm not married."

"What you mean?"

"Right now I'm so tired, I wish I had somebody to bathe me, dry me, carry me to bed and just hold me as I sleep."

"Oh Lord, preach it sister—preach it!"

This was one of the reasons I kept so busy. I tried to keep my mind off the base desires especially because there were so many reminders and especially because of one individual who was dangling himself before me invitingly. Things climaxed near the end of my tenure and I think my Journal entries for the eleventh and twenty-seventh of May sums it up well.

May 11, 2008
I've been having some interesting times. True, I've not been keeping you up to date—not because I didn't want to, but because everything has been so hectic.

Last week Sunday the sisters at the Hall, had a party for me. I also received some presents. This week Saturday, I went to a dinner; and today, Sunday I was at a Bridal Shower. I have been told that there would be more dinners for me—it has been good.

There will be no school tomorrow because of the damage done by the tornado in Bertie and other areas. I am glad, but hope they won't want us to make up this day. We have to make up two days already as it is...

The Watchtower study article was very interesting. It is especially encouraging for me at this time because of what I'm going through. No one would believe the pressure that I am under.

So often we put on our face and meet the world which simply takes things at face value. I look at people and wonder what demons they have to battle, even as they provide a smile or an encouraging thought for me.

May 27, 2008
We had to make up that day and we still have another to make up. Just think, three Saturdays in one month! I will just have to push myself.

There are all sorts of stuff lined up for Saturday: school, picnic for the soon-to-be-wed, dinner and then there is ...

He called me and emailed me. This frequency of communication was getting too much for my liking. I saw the harm in it and I saw the reminders, warnings and encouragements that Jehovah was providing, but I'm not responding well, I'm afraid.

When I read the Examining the Scriptures Daily, about Jehovah responding to prayers and looking on in secret, I cried. I am aware that what is happening to us is not pleasing to Jehovah.

He is a man with a knot. He desires me, but he can't have me. I am not available to him. He is kind and charming and I need both. That text he sent me with that endearment almost melted my heart. I have that need, as I have been created with, for love and to be treated with tenderness, but I can't accept his advances, his promises, or his threats.

It's good that I leave soon. I can't bear being around him. I have been trying hard to avoid him. He's open and makes no bones about how he feels… There's only so much of that stuff that a poor girl can take. I reminded him of my personal and spiritual positions. He apologized, promised that he would never do or say anything to disrespect me or hurt me, but not long after, he picked up where he left off.

The last time we had to work together, he wanted to touch me. I wouldn't let him, but I wanted him to… I didn't think it could get worse, but it did.

He came to my classroom. I was alone. When I looked up at him, I was alarmed by what I saw in his eyes. He came and stood near me and my body was experiencing some strange feelings. I don't know if the tremor was fear, desire or guilt—perhaps all three. I didn't want to let on to him how I was feeling and I hoped my eyes weren't as revealing as his. I had to remain firm for Jehovah's sake, since my reason was leaving me.

He held me, as I got up to move away. I won't say what I felt when he pulled me against him. I felt sorry for him.

I walked away and it took every ounce of my strength. I could not have run if I wanted to. He sounded desperate when he said, "Don't look!" My feet froze, then like Lot's wife, I looked anyway.

Turning, I saw what he was doing. I know I should have felt disgust, but I think I felt sorry for him. Going back, touching him was out of the question. I wish there was something I could do. I was torn between his pain and being faithful to God. I know that I should run away like Joseph, but I couldn't. Like Dinah, I stayed. I watched his back until I saw the tension eased away.

He had stopped quivering and even looked bashful. He smiled from where he was and said in a hoarse whisper, "Don't be afraid, baby girl." I'd never seen anything quite like that before.

After he left, I lowered myself in a chair and realized that I was shaking. When I realized that it was pointless to try and do any work I packed my things and managed to get to the car. It was as if my heart had just learned of what had happened. I collapsed into the car seat. I clutched the steering wheel, and whispered a brief prayer for forgiveness for what I'd witnessed. I waited for my heart to slow.

Can you believe that this is one of the things that I ran away from? Proverbs 22:3 is right. "Shrewd is the one that has seen the calamity and proceeded to hide himself, but the inexperienced have passed along and must suffer the penalty."

Here I was suffering the penalty of seeing too much, of not running when I should. Although my fear of displeasing God had made me stop the advances, I did not turn away fast enough. Was it stupidity or self-confidence? There is no way to put fire in your clothes and not burn your flesh. The searing heat in my core at that point was a poignant reminder.

Rousing myself, I started the car and headed out. The Bob Marley CD kicked in and tried valiantly to lift my spirits. As if to meet it half-way, I tried to sing along. My eyes would not cooperate and gave up any pretence when Bob launched into "No Woman No Cry."

I pulled off the main road to the soft shoulder and simply allowed the tears to flow. These tears were like rain after a long period of drought. They were big, hot and salty. They coursed down my cheeks from sockets that were hot springs, and splashed on my arms which I had wrapped around myself as I rocked in an effort to ease my own pain.

He would later commend me for my strength. Ha! My strength—it was power beyond what is normal. I could not have done that in my own strength. It is the same source that had been preventing me from doing harm to those students who so callously abused me, so blatantly disregarded the rules of the school and displayed such disrespect of all forms of authority.

There were some different students though, students who were average or normal. They only needed some direction. Marvin and Jason were rap writers. I would watch them work their lines each time the class went to breakfast. They often whispered the lyrics, because they were littered with profanities.

"Do you realize that you could have better effect and reach more people if you made it clean?" I asked them.

"What're you talking about, Miss Wright? Rap has to be like this. You ever hear Tupac, The Game…?"

"And where are they now? Your music should reflect not mere depression and conflict, but life as you would like to see it. Even if you talk about the social issues, you can say it in language suitable for polite company. You've heard LL Cool J?"

"You's crazy, Miss Wright!"

"Really, I could rap without curse words."

"You can rap?"

"What's there to it? It's just talking in a rhythm." I knew there was more to it, but that would work for the moment.

"A'ite, go ahead then. Let's hear you."

I decided to go with one they could relate to, which I had written years before.

Come on, listen to me,
Hey don't think I'm in joke
If you stock up on drugs
You'll be unable to cope

You'll be left in the darkness
Only to grope
So face your problems
Don't depend on dope

Protection, security
It doesn't provide
So stuff like that
One should always avoid
It takes your ambition
Your dignity and pride
So as quick as you can
Put drugs aside

"It makes me high"
That's how some contend
But what a big sigh
To see the money they spend

They resort to stealing,
Prostitution and say
It's in order that
They'll be able to pay
Yet in all of this
Not once did they say
"It's wrecking my life. It doesn't fit
It's wrecking society. Let's be done with it

Why don't you try
And copy Jesus Christ
He was offered drugs
Near the end of his life

Yet, he did refuse
Drug abuse—
He never chose

So leave off swallowing
Injecting
Forget about sniffing
And smoking
Hey I'm serious
I'm not joking
Can't you see
What
Is happening
Our young people's lives are going.

They had picked up the rhythm by the second stanza and were beating it out on the desk, adding their voice boxes for procession every now and again. They were very impressed and started to tell each other that I was better than the other. I pointed out to them that it was done in English, had no curse words and yet it explored the social problem of drug abuse and its effects on the individual and the larger society. I also helped them to see how they could become better rap writers if they were to master English as a subject. Those two boys became more interested in the literary analysis after that day.

I thought of one of my best writers who I lost because he was expelled. He had discharged a gun on the school property. I learned about the gangs that students were members of and watched them signing to each other each day. It saddened me as I watched some girls clutching their books against their growing stomachs and I wonder where the cycle would stop.

When I had the SAT group, I had difficulty getting them to write and complete their assignments. The school's star footballer asked me whether I had seen the movie *Blood Diamond*. Since I was trying to reach them, I decided to watch it and write a review of it. I wanted them to see that the content for their essays was in all these things they view, listen to and observe. They simply needed to apply the skills they were learning to compose their thoughts. He read the essay to the class. Then I asked them all to analyze the essay in light of their own experiences and perception of the movie. For that moment, they were all able to express their views in a focused way. They identified the main ideas and technique I used.

A Critical Review Of: "Blood Diamond"

"Blood Diamond" is a movie presented by the Warner Brothers Pictures. It is an R-rated (strong violence and language) film, directed by Edward Zwick and produced by Paula Weinsten, et al. The movie is set in the African country of Sierra Leone, a place being torn apart by: a desperate struggle for power, greed, political instability, civil war and a thriving underground diamond business.

The feature opened with a scene which is covered in darkness. This scene is soon broken by the light from a single match struck by Solomon Vandy, who is played by Djimon Hounsou. It presents the dream of this humble Mende fisherman who works daily to provide for his family and hopes that his son will one day become a doctor. This was to be the last day they had as an ordinary family.

Later that day, as the child returned from school, members of the R.U.F. (Revolutionary United Front) entered the village, robbing and causing mayhem. The family became separated and Solomon was taken to the mines to work. Ironically, he was spared for the same reason others lost their arms. The rebels would say, "The future is in your hand—no hand, no future." With this saying, they would cut off the right hand so they could not vote for the government. Because Solomon had strong arms, he was taken to slave in the diamond mine.

The Africans slave in the dirty river bed was juxtaposed with the white men dressed in their business suites discussing in measured tones, the problem of illegal diamond trade. Later, the problem was revealed to be even greater as it became clearer the extent of the corruption. Danny Archer, played by Leonardo DiCaprio, met Solomon in prison and learned of his find of a rare pink diamond of immense value. Danny was a vital part of the smuggling ring of diamond for arms. Having gotten his own release, he secured Solomon's and from there it was a quest to recover the diamond and Vandy's son who had been conscripted as a child soldier.

As the men traversed the country, devastated by the rebel forces which were brutally ravishing the people, the movie takes on an even deeper meaning. It becomes more obvious how men's greed and corruption can turn their hearts to be unfeeling. It is also this moment that reveals the deepest truths about the human condition. Archer's desire to get the diamond is balanced by Solomon's yearning to get back his family and especially his son. It was heartening to hear him cry, "My son is down there; I should have protected him." and to hear him ask simply, "How can my own people do bad things to each other?" It was later reinforced by Archer's gesture to return the diamond and to make arrangement for Solomon's safety.

David Denby in, *The New Yorker,* described the movie as being "spectacular, exciting and stunningly well made." I agree with this summary and would go on to say that it takes the viewer through a variety of emotions for the one-hour-and-forty-three minutes that it lasts. It was not superficial, as it explored many social issues such as: the civil war, the displacement of families and thousands of people who become refugees, the use of children for soldiers and the other problems of big businesses' involvement in supporting these rebels directly or indirectly.

After the discussion, he smiled and said, "You really didn't have to write me a review, Miss Wright."

"I know, but I did. So you see you too should be able to do your assignments in spite of your other commitments."

"Well, that's true I guess."

I left it at that.

As teachers, we were always trying different things to let the students see that we were interested in them and wanted them to learn. The group of us, Jamaican teachers, went to their games. This meant staying back after school because it was too much trouble to travel home over twenty miles away, and back. The games would be the place to meet parents too, as many of them would attend games even if they would not come to see you or call about their children. I am just sorry that it will take them a long time to realize all the sacrifices we were making for them, all the effort we made to meet them a part of the way.

CHAPTER ELEVEN

School Bullies: Students, Parents and Administrators

I have often accused the US of being a reactive society. For the most part they wait until the wagon comes along, then they all jump on it. For the week or so, they have their seven days of wonder—the more sensational, the better—and then the novelty wears off and it's on to the next sensation.

Recently, bullying was shot into the lime light by the deaths of two boys. They both killed themselves after being tirelessly bullied by their schoolmates. It is lamentable that such a thing should happen and I can understand how those boys felt before making that decision. From these separate tragedies, the public was treated to some staggering statistics. We learned that sixty-five percent of all teens are being bullied and that thirty-nine states have anti-bullying laws. They aptly define bullying as being "abnormal, unnatural and unnecessary." It is a conscious attempt to harm somebody. The bully gets pleasure from it and feels no guilt in the process. As usual, the poor teachers are blamed and accused of aiding and abetting or doing nothing to prevent it.

My mother is in the habit of using a rather interesting phrase: "Finger say look dey it no say look ya. But member oh, when you a point so, three fingers a point back on you." The society points accusingly at teachers, but they are guilty of bullying teachers too. The classroom teacher gets the worst of it. They are blamed for tolerating bullying in schools and they are bullied by children, parents, administration and then some. Yes, workplace bullying in school is so widespread it would make your head spin if you tried to fathom it. Sadly, it is accepted as normal and the victims may not even realize it until it is too late.

We, teachers, make ideal targets because we are, in general, good people who are often forgiving and ready to accept others and think the best of them. We are trained to be that way. We make allowances for people's conduct and will even excuse them for the sake of peace and progress.

Bullying has nothing to do with size or age, but everything to do with power, support and strategy. Within the school they learn to divide and rule. They get their power from scheming, plotting and pitching people against each other. Their lies and sometimes indirect negative impressions conveyed to others in authority often disarm and isolate their victim, the poor teacher. They pretend to be charming and respectable, but they operate like sugars that melt their way into your mouths and start or hasten decay. Initially, they work at breaking down trust. Then they produce uncertainty by their twisted remarks. Others in authority will believe them because they are usually convincing and they get more power by those who fail to make their own unbiased examination of events.

The decay would have started. The victims start to lose credit, self-esteem and would soon start to doubt their own abilities.

Feelings of humiliation and a lack of confidence soon follow as their self doubt grows. They believe what they hear because some of it is true. The bully would have eagerly listened to their impressions and stored these so that they can retrieve them later and use them as other devious strategies. Before I tell you how I endured as a target, I must make this important point: If the administration is efficient, powerful and effective, then bullying is unnecessary.

I speak extensively about teachers being bullied by administration, because I am convinced that the students who bully teachers may succeed with tacit support from management. From the few accounts I relate from my Jamaican teaching experience, you know that it occurs there too. For now, I will focus on my US experience, since it is more recent and more blatant here.

The location of my classroom and the combination of students placed in it were not helpful in my situation. When the nit-picking and the over-scrutiny started, it did not help either. But it was the feedback from the children that really set it alight.

By the third week of the second semester I was becoming used to being called, "bitch," the N-word and "a mad --- @#&%," among other names.

When I got a 'promotion' on February 14, we were still trying to enforce the uniform rules. A girl wearing a red blouse, came in just as we were about to start. I looked at her and decided I'd give her an option because I didn't want another "love letter" from Mr. Early. They had raided the class and had taken out some students who were not properly attired. Then they wrote to tell us how disappointed they were and that the offence would go on our files. Therefore, I was trying to avoid another incident.

"Miss Cherry, I'm going to suggest that you go to the office and get a pass to keep on that blouse in class." I advised. Secretly, I hoped they wouldn't give her one, but that day I didn't want the confrontation.

"What? You talking to me? No—you can't be—you better not be! This is my blouse and I'm a keep it on!"

"If you wish to keep it on, you can't stay in the classroom and that's the rule. So, I'll have to write you up."

"Yo, you want me to get ma Mama to come out here and cuss you out? I ain't leaving and I ain't taking off my blouse either!" She pulled it further down over her white uniform top in order to emphasize her point.

I began to write the referral. She turned to her friends for support and they all started. She was loudest.

"How come the other teacher don' say notton. What's 'e matter with you? It's Valentine's Day ho'!"

After I had submitted the referral, I was uneasy. It was not until later that I realized what I had done wrong. I called Mrs. Sanderson.

"Mrs. Sanderson, I have the uneasy feeling that I misspelled 'whore.' I think I left off the 'w'. I tell you, I doubt that I have ever written that word before so please understand my shock at being labeled as such."

I don't know if that girl was ever punished. ISS room was packed with senior students who were serving time there and I was told that the student would have to wait until there was room. I said nothing. The girl continued with her abuse and refusal to complete her tasks.

A few weeks later, the same class, but another student, a regular in ISS or OSS went overboard once again. They were asked to write a letter to a friend explaining what they had learned in the class up to that point and how the information had affected them. This was one of my methods of evaluating their progress and reviewing how much we had covered in the Pacing Guide. She wrote that she had not learned anything because that woman had her sent to ISS for no reason and that the teacher was a Jamaican and she was crazy and you know how those banana boat people are and she went on…

Like so many of my other issues with students, it was Mr. Ocheato who got the letter. He said, "But this is disrespectful. Let me have it." That was the last I saw or heard of it.

It was he and Mr. Longley who had come to my class when I first became aware of his tactics. They had arrived after lunch and the students were trying to give the impression that they were good, hard working students. It must have been Mr. Longley that they were trying to impress because he stood out as a white man and he was not from the school. In their effort to appear diligent, they created the opposite effect and overcompensated, because even after they had been given enough time, they were insisting that they were still on task.

Mr. Ocheato called me up after the visit. He wormed his way around, employing all the bullying technique I told you about. He talks a little like The Terminator, but he is about half that size.

"Miss Wright, you have to take back your class. The students are in control. I wrote your evaluation for the agency last week and you know what I said? I said that Miss Wright has the *potential* to be a great teacher. You heard that? *The potential!*" he laughed.

"Sir, I understand. I know that I am not operating at the level I want to, but you, in the office, need to give me the support. These students say I can write them up if I want because nobody in the office will do anything. They say I'm wasting paper."

"They say that? Well, you send them to me and I'll take it from there. It's the same way with Miss Luisa and Miss Bryant. They can't control their classes. Especially Miss Luisa, she come crying to me and I tell her, 'You have to take back control from the students—be a girl scout. Plan and carry out.'"

"But, sir, you must understand that because of the problem with poor behavior among the students, they often miss school or class. It is almost impossible to progress because the composition of the class keeps changing. No real learning is taking place among some of them. How do you think we can plan and progress?"

We talked for awhile and he promised to make his presence felt. Later he wrote me a letter listing the suggestions we had agreed on. I would buy a stop clock; change the desks around to

SCHOOL BULLIES: STUDENTS, PARENTS AND ADMINISTRATORS

face the chalkboard, even if it means that those on one side will have difficulty seeing all of the chalkboard. I put those things in place and they broke the clock in the second week.

While he was telling us to apply the rules and take control, he was saying in the staff meetings: "Some of you teachers send the students to the office for minor offences. You need to find ways to deal with this. Expletives are just a part of the culture." Obviously he never heard the account of how a war was lost because of the want of a horseshoe nail. Little wonder we weren't able to reach the students.

The school rules say what offences are not to be tolerated and the punishment that should be meted out. The students are not ignorant of these procedures and the consequences. When management tells them differently and taps them on the wrists or does nothing at all, they are undermining our position and confusing the issue. How dare he question our ability to remain in control!

I understood that it could have been frustrating to deal with some students or even some teachers at times, but they should really rethink their policies. Sometimes the teacher and administration were not on the same page.

I had a boy who was a problem from the start. I had listened to and cried with his mother. She was in a second marriage and the boy was not handling it well. He was susceptible to peer pressure and would do anything for attention, including getting a cast on his foot when it was not broken. He wore his pants down and pulled his underpants up. This looked ridiculous, because the pants fitted well, so he had to spend most of the time pulling them down, rather than up, as is usually the case. He cursed like the proverbial sailor and his parrot. When I told one teacher about the student, he said, "He reminds me of the Virginia Tech shooter. He's just a dumb ass kid." The other children would dare him to do things and he would do them. They dared him to come and ask me whether I was wearing a thong. I looked in his glossy blue grey eyes as the light and confusion danced there. I really felt sorry for him.

I said, "Just go and tell them to pay you. You did as they dared."

He was such a robot. There were days when he pushed me near the edge. He wanted to be sent home and I wanted to keep him in school. I was hoping to let him spend a week in school for a change. When he refused to stop cursing and the other students began to cry out injustice since they weren't allowed to curse, I was left with no choice. I wrote the referral and explained the situation.

When I saw Mrs. Sanderson she said, "Miss Wright, Jonathan was sent home."

"Oh, man, not again!" I had reacted out of frustration.

"What else you want me to do, Miss Wright?"

I apologized and she walked down the hall. I didn't want him to be sent home. That was what he wanted. It was not helping anybody, but how could I explain it? I felt as though I was failing him. The only two times I saw that boy display any real interest were when he offered to weld my stool and when we were exploring the effects of war. His father was in the military and his grandfather had fought in Vietnam. I had asked him to write an essay explaining the welding process then graded it. It was the only work I ever got from him.

There were many incidents when individual students were abusive or attempted to be intimidating. But it was especially hard to bear when adults were involved, but they didn't seem to be objective.

I was passing Mrs. Burns' office one afternoon, when I paused to greet her. When I looked in, I noticed that one of my students was with her. I got the funny feeling that all was not well and enquired. She was actually making a report against me. I was livid.

"You mean to tell me that you have a problem with me, but thought it best to report it to Mrs. Burns before you came to me?"

"I came to you, but you didn't grade the whole paper, Miss Wright."

"Didn't I return the paper to you and ask you to redo the task? Haven't I graded the second attempt and showed it to you?"

"Yes, but you didn't grade the ones on the back!"

"So, who do you think is in a better position to mark it, me or Mrs. Burns? You are being unfair. If you saw that I failed to mark the whole thing, you could have brought it to my attention. Just remember I am human. I make mistakes too. Moreover, it was I who gave you a second chance. What would I stand to gain by robbing you?"

Mrs. Burns asked her to go and proceeded to tell me about the girl's position. She had two children and needed to maintain a "B" average in order for the state to keep paying the nursery fee for the babies.

"If she knows that, she should be making the effort to keep up those grades. She is often absent and sometimes it is the second chance that is saving her. This is SAT—it is chiefly Multiple Choice and Writing. I can't make a student pass. You realize how difficult it is to grade papers twice?"

The student's mother would call me one day after school to "cuss me out." She wanted to know if I was going to come and babysit the children when the daughter failed to keep up her grades. I asked her if she expected me to give grades for the sake of the babies or should the girl earn her grades? She would hear nothing from me. I stopped trying to defend my position or help her see sense and allowed her to rant then I wished her a good day.

All through my previous thirteen years in the school system, I did not witness one fight in my classroom. I had two major fights in the ten months in NC. There were other fights involving my students, but those were not while they were with me. The first fight started with the usual teasing and bullying. Only, it was hard to tell who was bullying who at times. The students called each other "gay," "nigger" and other names based on afflictions or deficiencies. Sometimes the boys would pretend to be boxing and I would simply prevent it from becoming too rough—children play.

Because Mr. Ocheato had asked that the desk be turned around, so that all faced front, Ryan was out of my range of vision if I was at the chalkboard, thanks to that projection of the wall into the classroom. Warren had just spoken to me and had returned to his seat, when Ryan came up to me panting.

"So you not goin' do noting bout dat?"

"What?" I asked confused.

"You didn't see him slap me?" I thought of all the other days when he had slapped other boys, then they all asked not to be written up because they were only playing. But this time he was not playing and I did not see or hear the slap in question.

"Ryan, calm down a bit please. Let me finish here, then I'll deal with the matter."

He continued to argue noisily and began to threaten Warren. I asked another boy to take the referral to the Office and encouraged Ryan to go with him and explain what had happened. I walked with them to the porch and then turned and went back into the classroom to get the class together so we could continue.

The next thing I knew there was a big commotion. Ryan had raced back into the classroom and plunged into Warren's stomach head first, clawing and punching. It ended as quickly as it had started. But like a freak storm, what damage! Ryan then burst open the back door—with screws flying any which way—and Warren went through the front. They were both arrested.

I had to meet with both mothers. Where are the fathers of these students? Warren's mother was understanding because we had been in dialogue before and we had been working to keep Warren in school and focused on his schoolwork. Ryan's mother on the other hand, had come to do battle with me. This was not about her son. Oh no! It was about this inept teacher who had gotten her darling baby in trouble. If the teacher had responded to all his complaints and stopped the bullying of her dear son, things would not have gotten this far. In the meantime, the son was pouting and telling her to stop. After all, he knew the truth.

She started on another topic. Why was her baby, who used to do so well suddenly failing English? I wondered whether she knew that the boy couldn't write an effective paragraph and had no desire to be corrected. I tried to explain to her that if students don't work they don't get grades. I was not sure what some of the other teachers were doing as students boasted about doing nothing and still passing their classes. Students had to earn their grades in my class and these grades should be above question. When she failed to get what I was saying, the Dean of Discipline, who was with us at the time, told her what I meant in his own words which were unequivocal. She dropped the subject, but promised to remove the boy from my class. He insisted on staying because he was getting his work done. Warren had to repeat the class and Ryan barely passed. I don't know what became of the court case.

The second fight was in Second Semester. It occurred in the first block. This class had some big students. I'm careful about when I used the word "big." Once in this same class, I had put my foot in my mouth with these students. I had said that I expected better behavior from a student because he was a big boy. He wanted to know what size had to do with it. Before the class ended I was being threatened with a lawsuit. I learned not to mention their sizes, even if they were obviously big—especially when they were obviously big.

SCHOOL BULLIES: STUDENTS, PARENTS AND ADMINISTRATORS 225

My class had several EC students. They are sometimes called special students. They had all sorts of challenges and I had to learn to deal with them, adjust my instructions and grades and deal with whatever behavioral problems they displayed. Thanks to the No Child Left Behind policy. One of my students, Bryan, had a sleeping disorder and he was on meds. I was told that he might fall asleep sometimes and when that occurred, I could allow him to sleep.

On this day in question, he had finished his work and was asleep. As I moved around the room, I noticed some pieces of crackers on the floor near his desk. I asked that someone remove it. Apparently, James took up the crackers and threw it on Bryan. The other students said there was a pre-existing problem. Bryan woke up and an argument ensued. I spoke to them, but they paid no attention. When I saw that the situation was getting volatile even after I had spoken to them, I called the office.

Bryan was well over two hundred pounds and James was loitering in that region. But these boys are footballers, so we are talking about muscles here not just flabs. It was raining and as the tension grew so did the anticipation. There was lightning outside, the action was about to start and there was a video recorder, and many phone cameras running. A few were trying to separate them, because they were now getting in each other's face.

Mr. Ocheato had just entered the door and was in the process of closing his umbrella when it started. He dropped the umbrella and rushed in the melee. They were like two hippopotami and a gazelle. He got in the middle and was just as easily dashed aside. As all three of them landed on the floor, his pants ripped open. They were up again in a flash and he was clinging on like a rock badger. The boys were punching each other from one side of the room to the back, down the middle and to the front. The Sheriff and Mr. Early arrived and joined in the fray. They were locked at the telephone, still pushing in a punch, but nobody willing to give up. They were too tied up to throw their arms. They were like too weary boxers against the ropes in the corner of the ring.

The Sheriff was threatening to pull his stun gun. The telephone was bleeding and so were the boys. Mr. Early managed to lock James' arms behind him in one of those wrestler's holds. He forced him to the desk and James was bending over and Mr. Early was practically on his back. Now Mr. Early was a coach and he is well toned and seemed strong, but he was no match for James. That boy was snorting like a bull. He broke away and was going after Bryan again. Mrs. Sanderson was also on the scene. It took some big boys, three principals and a Sheriff to get two mad boys under control.

Of course, I was trembling. I made sure that I was standing out of the way. I had been emailed the account of the young man who joined Teach for America and got sued for twenty million dollars because of a student's and a parent's accusations and false allegations of abuse when he tried to help. I was too near the end to let them ensnare me in a lawsuit or half-kill me.

Students had received text messages and phone calls and raced to the center of the action before the group left the room. Mr. Ocheato went home and changed his pants. The boys were carted off to be arrested. Once again I had to endure the abuse of a parent who thought that somehow, her angel had been misguided by a bad teacher.

James' mother and I had recently met and discussed some changes she had observed in her son. She had come the morning after they had an altercation at home in which she had gotten physical with him. So, although she was disappointed, she was not at all surprised. Bryan's mother was another matter. She was so busy blaming me that she failed to see how her son could have been culpable. June could not come too soon, I told myself.

When Mr. Seamer, a social worker at the school, heard about the incident, he went to ask Mrs. Burns whether he could sit in my room sometimes to help to maintain the peace. He said that she told him to take the yellow writing pad and take notes of his observations. He came one day and didn't last five minutes. They called him names, hurled insults, abuses and back talks. He ordered two students to go with him to the office and that was that. The students returned smiling. He didn't return at all and I didn't hear what happened.

Some long time after that, I saw him and we began to talk. He explained to me how his authority had been undermined before the students that day in the office.

"Welcome to the club." I said, "The students tell me that if I want them to respect me, I have to cry like Miss Hunter. I tell them they will never live so long."

"Did they really say that Miss Wright? But they are horrible!"

"They say a whole lot more. They gave me a list of teachers who are not respected at the office. The other day I refused to listen to them speak badly about two teachers and they told me that the teachers didn't mind when they talked about me and other teachers before them."

"Really, we are defeating ourselves, Miss Wright. Ooh, we're beating ourselves—Jesus um-um."

"I know. I told them that people have to learn to live by their own integrity and I would never tolerate that kind of talk about my colleagues."

"Miss Wright, how do you endure it?"

"I think I tend to look at how the greatest teachers operated. Jesus taught even as the audience mumbled, complained and threatened to kill him. His disciples who were really interested sought him out after for clarifications. He did his job. He was perfect, but he didn't have a perfect class and even he got physical and stressed by his situation. I just laugh at the likes of this administration that is projecting their inefficiencies on us."

"You are so right. I never looked at it that way."

"I watch them—the children, go crazy sometimes and I smile. I think of Satan. He rejected the greatest personage in the universe, so who am I to take offence when these students act up as they do? Another thing I do that really consoles me is this scripture in Exodus when Jehovah told Moses, 'I have looked at this people and here it is a stiff-necked people. So now leave me be that my anger may blaze against them and I may exterminate them.' I take comfort in the fact that I can't save the world. I have limits."

"Wow, does the Bible really say that? I really must read it some more."

"Boy, I don't know what I would do without it. It helps me to recognize my limitations and keep things in perspective."

"That is so important."

It is easy to stay in the stands and criticize a player's ineptitudes on the field of play, but it is another matter when you are on the field and the pressure is on you. Barack Obama learned this from his own experience as he related in his book, *Dreams from My Father*. When Johnnie, his friend, said to him, "I don't know Barack, sometimes I'm afraid of 'em. You got to be afraid of somebody who just doesn't care. Don't matter how young they are." Barack said, "Was I afraid? I didn't think so…" But not long after when he was confronted by some young boys in a car at night, he said: "I turned back toward my apartment … knowing that I am afraid after all."

Sometimes that is all it takes, a moment of vulnerability to remind us of how human we are and how we can be intimidated in a particular setting. It is especially true if we are brave enough to challenge the self-esteem of these children in an effort to stimulate their appetite to learn. While you are not invincible, and you know you don't want to be kept captive by fear, you have to recognize the source and potential of your own power. This in turn, will make you experience true freedom.

So those students, who wondered why I smiled when they cursed at me, please know that I had not lost my senses. Rather, I knew my power. My power enabled me to do the one thing I needed to do–survive.

CHAPTER TWELVE

Observations, Evaluations and the Teacher's Response

The Program was very explicit in its object to source the best teachers internationally for the districts that need them. When we were recruited, we knew that our objective was to internationalize education. The agency was of the view that the schools' curriculum didn't have to be overhauled in order to implement global themes. I can't speak for the other subjects, but I got enough feedback that I can say it was easy to adapt the themes in order to make students both culturally and internationally aware.

As for English, by all rights, we should have had a field day. Culture is not something we have done incidentally, it was written in the State's Curriculum. In Jamaica, I taught my students about the impact of globalization and the importance for them to acquire an education that would prepare them for any job, anywhere in the world. I was not content to teach them the Jamaican Standard English, but helped them to accept and value the Jamaican Creole. I tried to help them to appreciate both the British and American English Language and Literature. It may seem redundant, but when I had them listen to the sound track from "My Fair Lady", many started to pay attention and appreciate that there were different standards of English. One simple example I use is the pronunciation of WATER.

    Britain: wa'a   USA: wader   JA: wata

They would be amused by the idea and would listen to themselves say the words. They admitted that language was fascinating and dynamic. They soon learned some of the other words that were different.

Here is where tolerance is taught. They need to accept that different is not always or necessarily wrong, but if not used in the correct context, may be considered inappropriate. My students knew that in Jamaica we use the British grammar and spelling. They were also made aware of the American spelling and pronunciations. This was an aspect of the transmission of culture. They also developed an awareness of the effect of globalization.

I had some interesting experiences when this aspect of my knowledge and culture conflicted with those of the American students. I concluded that somebody had not done a good job of preparing these students. They did not get the idea that the United States is not the world. This contributed to the intolerance that the students showed to other cultures. I remember some conflicts in class that cause me to chuckle to this day.

I had written some instructions on the transparency for the overhead projector. The students were in the process of copying it when our little friend of "banana boat" fame said: "Where you come from, you don't speak English? I don't know why you here. You can't even spell. There is no word as 'PRACTISE'. How you say that prack-tize? You dumb, Miss Wright. Sorry, but that's not a word."

"Now, that is why I encourage you to be friends with your dictionary. If you were to check your dictionary, it would tell you that PRACTISE is a verb and PRACTICE is a noun. It is true that the Americans have simplified things by just using one word for both parts of speech, but the British use them separately. So we say, 'It is his PRACTICE to PRACTISE on the lawn every day.' Just remember C for cat, a noun and S for sat the verb. Even if you're not using them in writing, it helps to know so that you don't have someone getting the last laugh on you."

One student went even further in her criticism of me and my methods. "You're a lame excuse for a teacher. In fact there are only two English teachers in this here school, they be Mrs. Williamston and Mrs. Spacecraft." Both of these teachers were Americans.

When Mrs. Williamston came to my room during my planning and read the objectives on the board she made an observation. It makes me think of her every time I see the word "learned." She said, "Darling, you have LEARNED there, but you mean LEARNT. You see, we use LEARNED to mean 'having great learning', but you want this to mean the past tense of learn."

Out of deference to her years of experience, I made the adjustment, but I also knew that the verb learn has the past tense LEARNT or LEARNED, pronounced LURNT. However, LEARNED is also an adjective, which is pronounced LER-NID. It was necessary to make concession where there was no major life-altering principle involved. The students were another matter.

They had no reason to object, except their ignorance and desire to be mean.

We would have those arguments often with the students, because they didn't read enough to see publications from other English-speaking countries and so they were unaware of these little differences in the language. I thought it was important to help them to accept these things, so as to give them hope. They thought it was just evidence of my ignorance and inability to teach. They needed to develop their minds and explore the world apart from their own. I tried to help them to do so vicariously.

The full-color wall map provided by the agency was indispensable to my teaching. The literature we studied in class was chiefly from other countries and we pretended to be visiting each country. We started with the story, *The Bracelet.* This story is set in France, so we went to France. We explored several themes and the students were taught how to develop a theme by selecting words or phrases from different parts of the story to create a central idea. This developed their skill in close reading for main idea and allowed the students to *find a poem*. They were very excited by this concept and here is what some of them found.

> ***The Bracelet***
>
> *Twenty-nine square pave diamonds*
> *Twenty-nine square brilliants*
> *All set in a bracelet*
> *A hundred iridescent rainbows*
> *Blue sparks blazing with color*
> *The bracelet*
>   *D.C.*
>   *09-06-07*

Once Young

A little ten year old girl wearing on her wrist a bracelet of blue glass
All she saw was a round piece of bluish glass

Madame Augelier thus came to know how old she really was
Madame Augelier raised her hand, tucked her little finger under,

Extended her wrist to ease the bracelet of wrinkles
A shudder made Madame Augelier's slack cheeks tighten
Her prematurely white hair, which she did not dye, appeared even whiter as she adjusted amid slightly frizzy curls

The vision ended and Madame Augelier fell back, bruised, into the present, into reality
Resigned, to know how old she really was.

D. D.
03-14-08

They were expected to compose and illustrate these poems and they did. You were probably thinking that after these fights and conflicts that we did nothing, but argue each day. We did quite a bit and could have done a whole lot more if the conditions were conducive. It's just that it took so much to get so little done that sometimes I wondered whether it was worth it.

We read "*The Guest*", by Albert Camus after this story because it is set in Algeria. This setting was significant to them because Madame Augelier's husband is said to be in Algeria. We were off to Africa. Again the matter of culture came to the fore as they were able to see how the Arabs behaved and compared it to the school teacher and the police who were French men with different perspectives based on their own experiences and individual culture. We explored the themes of existentialism and attitude to power and authority and how the setting of the Sahara affected them. To reinforce these themes we watched the DVD, *Happy Feet,* which is set in the Antarctic and then used the Double-Bubble Thinking Maps to compare and contrast the themes, settings and other elements.

Since we were in Africa, we decided to go over to Nigeria. So we read *Civil Peace* and I allowed them to come home briefly because they had to research conflicts. They had to complete a group project in which they looked at: War for Independence, the American Civil War, the War on Terror and East vs. West conflict. The students in the first semester were even able to engage in a cultural competition in Education Week. They selected a country, and then presented information on the people, language, clothes, music, food etc. This was displayed on a poster board and judged. The prize was money and grades. I got judges from outside the groups

While they were reading stories and watching films, they were also developing their writing, vocabulary, language and usage skills. They would write and conduct interviews as well as write advertisements, short arguments and present them. When they protested that the topic of The American Dream was "lame," I realized how much I had taken for granted. They had no idea what the American dream was about.

I went in search of and bought the DVD, *A Raisin in the Sun*. We got permission to watch it. We made notes about the dreams and aspiration of the Younger family and the obstacles to their fulfilling them, then the students related it to their own experience. They learned that not much had changed since the play was written, since these are still the dreams of the average person today all over the world, which makes the theme universal. We looked at the many different game shows on TV and talked about why they were so successful. They were also able to see how the desire to fulfill some of these dreams has led to the deadly sins. I was careful to keep the links and the main idea so they were encouraged to read Martin Luther King, Jr., "*I have a dream*" speech. Some of them were seeing the speech for the first time.

Soon it was time to go traveling again. This time we went to the West Indies. We went to Antigua through an excerpt from *Annie John,* entitled, *A Walk to the Jetty.* They met the author, Jamaica Kincaid, through viewing a DVD of an interview with her. Although the students in the SAT group were not doing this story, I still had them watch it because of how she lifted herself out of her poverty by acquiring an education. We did the history of how France colonized Algeria and England colonized Antigua and America and the result of this.

I was learning a great deal from these literatures, that I had not read before, about the students and how they were learning and what I wanted them to learn. I was so excited that I tried to get them to watch the news on what was happening in Kenya and Darfur. I could not get them curious. I asked whether they were following the Democratic race with Hillary Clinton and Barack Obama. After the Iowa Caucus, I asked if they had heard the debates.

The only comment was, "Let dat boy go sid down. He ai' go win notton!" I decided to let it go.

The Jena Six incident in Louisiana did create a stir—only a small stir, not a constructive extended argument. We seemed to do better when we were traveling. It was time to go back and so we went to Egypt with a group of love poems.

Many of these stories were either on CDs or audio cassettes. I had bought a player for both and would either play the stories, read them or have the students read. Second Block in the Second Semester taught me about "popcorn reading." In this game, one person reads, calls on another who pops up and reads and the game goes on. These little concessions helped to keep the peace in the classroom. I think it is only fair that they should have a say in how some of the activities are carried out since they have to do it. Learning involves both the teacher and the students so both parties should contribute to the process.

My first official evaluation was, in my view, long overdue. Since we were well along in the second semester and I had had at least two meetings with Mrs. Burns in which I had expressed my concerns and intention to resign, I thought someone would have come and given me some feedback on my practice. She had passed through, but I had not learnt anything from her observations. Therefore, I was rather pleased when she called to tell me that she was coming to see me—officially. I had to meet with her to fill out a form and select the day and time. My request on the form was for the classroom to be cleaned.

Although I was sweeping twice each day—I know the custodians at my old school will find this amusing—it was still filthy. When I informed the chief custodian, he kindly informed me that mine looked good when compared to Miss Bryant's. Yet, I would see them mopping the already shine corridors in the main building on a regular basis. There was one custodian who did a very good job. When he was finished it smelled fresh and showed the potential to shine. I did not have to go over. But he was a temp. The others merely gave it a promise to do better the next time.

I wanted her to visit with the second block, because this was my problem group of mainly girls. However, she had another appointment in that slot so we had to settle on the fourth block. This was a problem group of mainly boys. I gave her a copy of the lesson plan and went back to work to ensure that we would cover the other lessons to be at that point on the given day. We had been building toward writing an essay on war. Most of the stories were focused on one form of conflict or another.

One boy asked, "Miss Wright, did you have a lot of problems in Jamaica?"

"Not more than is normal, why?" I respond.

"Because you always talking about war."

"I realize how it may appear, but these are all in the Pacing Guide—I didn't make the list. We just have to try to find something positive in it, won't we?"

I was trying to have them write two essays on the same topic, both the definition and the cause-and-effect essays. I had them get the definitions on war from different sources. They were encouraged to go online to get quotations. They had to go to the library in groups of three and some used our little computer in the room. They said they didn't have internet at home and the library could not always accommodate all of them. Next, they had to formulate four questions they would like answered about war. With all this information, they had to create their own test questions based on past State Writing tests. I reasoned that if they went through the process, they would know how to approach and respond to these writing questions. All they needed at that point was the content. Here was where integration came in. We were going to consider the poem, *Thoughts of Hanoi,* which is set in Vietnam during the war.

When I told the first block about my wish to have an actual veteran, Bryan—yes, same Bryan, but before the fight, he suggested the Colonel in the JROTC. The boys in fourth block wanted Coach Major who was also in the army. Initially he agreed to do the fourth block since he would have had his planning, but something had come up. In the end it was the Colonel, who was willing, available and able. We were set. He was able to be with each class, so we would have him all day! All my students would be having a similar experience. We arranged for someone to escort him to class and for another student to say thanks at the end of the presentation. They could ask him the questions they had prepared or any that arose during the presentation.

The first two classes went well. The Colonel was on time and the students were well behaved. Some students even asked him for his view on their quotations in the context of his experience. Of course, the boys wanted to know if he had shot anybody in Vietnam. During the presentation I walked around and encouraged then to remain interested and to take notes. As usual, my second block had to put a spike in the wheel. One girl looked at me and asked: "When're you gonna teach us something around here?"

Because it was not confirmed that Colonel would return for the last class, I spent the best part of my lunch period trying to get things in place. I was over the moon when he agreed to come. He would be setting off his class before coming to us.

Mrs. Burns was on time. I took the class through the objectives which is often written on the board overnight. I helped to build anticipation for what was to come, and reminded them of what they were expected to do. We went through the agenda and there was still no sign of the Colonel. I explained that he had confirmed that he would arrive a little after so we would start the song until he arrived. It was *Buffalo Soldiers* by Bob Marley. They were encouraged to listen to the lyrics and see how they relate to our objectives. The Colonel marched in as Bob and the more convivial students' voices faded. They wanted to hear it again, but the show must go on. I introduced the gentleman who was late because he had gone to make copies of the Vietnam region, as well as notes on the war, for the class.

He launched into his presentation using the globe, making reference to his handouts and presenting statistics on the war as he explained how this war was still affecting the American society even today. There were some staggering figures that spoke to the toll it is taking on the health sector and how the economy was burdened by the new wars. We invited the students to think of some other areas of the society that could make better use of the money that has been diverted to fight. I was fascinated by the presentation. I moved around and helped the short attention spans to stretch a little more. I encouraged questioning, asking a few myself to keep the presenter focused. Even Mrs. Burns got involved generating interest among the students. I asked him to explain the song and say to what extent the events affected the African and American experience.

A man from the county's maintenance crew had come during second block to install a lock on the door that leads to the small room. Why? I don't know. He came back during the fourth block, during the class to finish. The phone rang four times. A student carried some report forms for the EC students. A rescue squad vehicle came along the window and by the back door with its siren blaring. When it became quiet, the JROTC squad came marching and chanting. We locked the door and in spite of all of what went on around us we kept our focus—amazing!

After the Colonel had finished his presentation, we thanked him and he was off. I took over by making the connection to the poem we were about to analyze. We would listen to the poem, I would read and they would read it also. The poem was read by a woman and a student wanted to know why she was breathing so deeply. We examined the poem and then reviewed the information gathered from the presentation, their research, the song and our discussion. At that point they were to start drafting their own letters. They were to imagine that they were living in a war torn country and write a letter to a friend, describing the effects of the war. Mrs. Burns left after viewing a few of the drafts. I supervised the drafts and graded the final product when they were done a couple days later. This was the best letter I received and it was the writer's third production.

February 14, 2008
Dear Chris,

Listen, I know in the past we have had our differences but that's in the past and let's leave it there. Being on opposing sides has made me think about what type of

OBSERVATIONS, EVALUATIONS AND THE TEACHER'S RESPONSE 243

friendship we have and I know that no matter what happends that nothing will change my mind. After all of this, what will become of our homes, and sites we've seen in our cities?

Honestly, I believe that it would be morally wrong to have to shoot my cousin over something like this. I mean, thinking about us going to school together everything we did and all the memories we have made. What will this do to our friendship just throw it away pretend like it doesn't matter. I can see already that such a pointless war has not yet ruined but put a strain on us. What do you think the outcome will be?

Not only that but think about our families and where we live, do you really believe that some of the soldiers who know that there only going kill all the opposing army are going to stop and leave your home alone? I mean, think about after the bombs, fires, and gun shots our homes wont still be there, nothing will be left but piles of rubble and mulch.

Another thing that will change is our cities and Land marks. The places around us are full of sites, parks, and important buildings. We have been in many buildings gone to many towns and seen so much and soon there will be nothing but memories, nothing to go back to. After this war we will have no cities, parks, sites, or buildings just dirt, fire, rock, smoke, and blood.

Look cuz, I don't want to die tomorrow and only have memories of the past. I don't want us to fight if it must be our final day and my death with you as my friend will bring me joy, but as my enemy will only cause me more pain. Why must we fight in this pointless war? Why must we die for such a pointless cause and lose all we know?

Sincerely,
H.

A month later I had not received any feedback from Mrs. Burns on the evaluation. Donna, June, Megan and others had been seen by other people and had received their feedback. I was concerned. I decided to go to Mrs. Burns.

"Mrs. Burns, I think I have good reason to be a little jealous," I told her.

"Why?" she asked somewhat curiously.

"Well, the others had their evaluations and are all excited and I still haven't gotten any feedback from you on my evaluation."

"Oh, I'm sorry. You know, I didn't write it up as yet. But I spoke to some of the students and Danny was saying you had not graded his work."

"But he had not followed instructions. We were writing letters describing the effects of the war and he had partially written a narrative that had nothing to do with what we were focused on."

"Okay, I wanted to see some of the finished work. Here," she reached down and took up the yellow writing pad from under a pile of papers on her desk, "you can look at what I have written."

I read her notes and was satisfied with the lesson. She had only two concerns and they were: Why is Devaun playing with the globe? She should have noticed that there was nowhere else to put it. He chose to rub it down. She also questioned the relevance of the song. I am sure she would have found out near the end of the presentation when we looked at the effect on the African population and society in general. How does a nation recover from the sudden removal of thousands of its most productive citizens? Then they came to participate in the genocide of the Natives of the Americas. The impact would be obvious and so is the relevance of the song. "Stolen from Africa, taken to America ... fighting on arrival, fighting for survival ..." So the song was explained thoroughly.

"It's not just that the speaker was late," she added. "I wanted to see you lecture some more."

All this sounded like a lot of you-know-what to me, but I decided to play along with it. I took a sample from each class from the highest, middle and lowest grades to her in a folder. She checked them and wrote her comments on the most outstanding ones and returned them to me. About the "lecture some more" bit, I thought, "Is this woman serious? In this day and age, who lectures for more than half-an-hour? Did she see and hear those students? How would we have covered all that in the allotted time? What would I have lectured about? We had covered the essential points for the lesson. The guest had spoken for about forty minutes; it would have been torture to have the students sit through another long presentation." She planned to see me again in April.

What would you have thought? There was not even a little commendation for how I carried on despite the distractions.

There was no lull in the class, and the interruptions did not significantly affect the presentations. I had kept it together and there was no comment on it. It's as they say: Some people take your confidence and they don't give it back—they can't.

Even after this I refused to be beaten. I had to call her to my aid one day. I had given out the Progress Report and the students were on the war path. I am not in the habit of fawning over children and I don't have pets in class. They have to earn what they get in class. Because I had given them the grades they had earned, some were hurling insults at me. I stood my ground and their bitter words fell on and around me like aerial arrows. I wish I could say they fell like water off a ducks back, but I was wounded by some of them. They started to make up all sorts of stories and to blow innocent incidents out of proportion.

Mrs. Burns came in and listened for awhile. I was listening to the students and responding to their concerns. They were questioning all sorts of things about my practices: make-up work, method of grading, method of teaching, country of origin and ability to speak, among other things.

This came to a head when 'Banana Boat' shouted, "She never teach us nothing. Why do we have to learn about existentialism anyway?"

By this time Mrs. Burns was helping to control the flow of conversation and deal with the concerns. I said, "Mrs. Burns, would you please explain to them that I have a Pacing Guide from the county board that I have to follow; therefore, I can't just teach what they want?" She explained this to them and the next question was directed to her.

"Why do we have to have a foreigner teaching us English?"

At this point Mrs. Burns asked me to go outside. I went and they closed the door. I don't know what was said. When they called me twenty minutes later, everyone was quiet. There were some notes on the board that had come out of their discussion.

I kept their work in folders in the filing cabinet. This was deemed necessary because they threw away the papers when they were returned and there was no point of reference for me. Sometimes parents would come by and this had to be produced to prove the child's activity in class. Some of them lied about completing tasks and so this kept both of us accountable. I would have to go through the class and pick them up after they left. They could look at the folders at any time.

They wanted letter grade or percentage instead of a fraction. These students would do anything so as not to think. What is going to happen to their brains if they don't train them? Another demand had to do with make-up grade. You know how I feel about this make-up grade already. My question was this: Can you recall and apply something you didn't learn? It means that make up work would be some work sheet that the other students didn't get. More marking and research for the already over-stretched teacher.

I should buy a notice board so that I could post homework and due dates on it. I told them that was pushing it. I was already buying air freshener, paper towels, hand sanitizer and treats. More over a notice board was not going to make them complete the homework which was already being written on the chalkboard below the objectives. They said other teachers did it and I told them that it was their business. Some of their requests were too much and unreasonable. They thought I was some superhuman or something; I was an average human. All these things they were putting me through would come back to haunt them. They laughed.

A few weeks later I was just about to start when Mr. Early walked in. I was right at the point of taking them through the objectives. This was the same second block.

I thought it odd when a girl asked, "What is she doing? She never did this before?" This is the same girl who had asked when I was going to teach them something around here. I thought she was referring to one of her friends. She called to one of her friends and asked her and winked.

"Oh, yea, what is she doing? She never done that before!"

The message went around the room quickly and soon they were all in on the plan. They didn't know anything because I never taught them anything and now that Mr. Early was there, I was going to pretend that I could teach. They laughed out loudly and whispered. They didn't know the answer to any of my questions or they shouted out some unrelated responses. After nearly forty minutes of this uphill battle, I gave up.

"Well, I guess I ought to commend you for not being hypocrites. You have been yourselves today with a little extra, I'd say. I hope that you are pleased with yourselves."

I could not hide the sarcasm. I was really hurt by their conduct. I have never been subjected to such hatred. I looked into their unsmiling eyes and was struck by the coldness there. I bemoaned the American society's future if they were the guardians of it.

When they were instructed to complete the written assignment, Mr. Early left. I felt defeated. I never thought it was possible for a whole class to orchestrate such a devious scheme. There was not one student to say, "Stop! Enough!" The only time I felt relieved was when the telephone rang and a parent came to the door about her child. Mr. Early said I should tell her to come back during my planning. He could not see how relieved I was to be out of the room.

After the session ended, I went and told Tonetta and we bemoaned the condition together. I went to the office to see Mr. Early, but he had gone to do his duties. I found Mrs. Spacecraft, who also had a bad day, and she and I went in search of Mrs. Williamston. When we got to her room, we heard that she was absent from school. Since her room door was opened, we went inside and sat down and tried to figure out how best to deal with these students and we vented our frustrations.

Mrs. Williamston felt sorry for us when she returned to work the following day and heard about our experiences. She was like a mad mother hen. Once again she marched to the office where she found the principals together and related to them what I told her. She asked Mr. Early whether I had known of his intent to visit my class. She asked whether I was prepared for class. All this was to establish the kinds of students that were in question. She told them again of her own experience with them, as well as the incident in which they claimed that they were not being taught, but questioned why they had to learn about existentialism and other themes we had covered. She tried to demonstrate that the students were being spiteful. I would receive this feedback from Mr. Early a few days later.

Teacher Observation Checklist
April 14, 2008
Objectives:

A check (√) indicates at standard. A negative (-) indicates below standard.
If an item is not marked, it was not observed during the observation.

Instructional Time
Materials √   *class started quickly* √   *Time on task for learning*

Narrative: Class began with a bell ringer. Class began quickly and students were initially engaged.

Student Behavior
Rules posted √   *Frequently monitors behavior*   *Stops inappropriate behavior*

Narrative: Most students are talking and off-task. Ms Wright attempts to correct them with little success. There are several students engaged in their own conversations. There is no evidence of class participation procedures or student movement procedures.

Instructional Presentation
Lesson objectives visible in classroom √   *Objectives stated at beginning of lesson*   √ *Links to prior learning* √
Makes content meaningful; relevant examples   *High rate of success on tasks*   *Brisk pace*
Effective, smooth transitions   *Adapts instructions to diverse learners*   *Assignment clear* √
Uses technology to support instruction   **Students engaged, responsible for learning**
Provides closure to lesson   **Develops critical thinking & problem solving skills**

Narrative: Miss Wright begins class with a bell ringer at 9:50. The bell ringer has not been completed by all students at 10:00. At 10:20 Ms. Wright is trying to bring closure to the bell ringer but the class is too disruptive and not paying attention. Ms. Wright lecture is well-organized but ineffective because of the disorder in the class.

Instructional Monitoring
Maintains deadlines, standards   Circulates to check students' performance
Poses questions clearly and one at a time √   Uses responses to adjust teaching

Narrative: Ms. Wright assessment strategies consisted of choral responses and volunteer questioning. Ms Wright did very little circulating during her lecture. Ms. Wright attempted to correct inappropriate behavior quickly but the students were very defiant and noncompliant.

Instructional Feedback
Prompt feedback on work products   Affirms correct response quickly √
Sustaining feedback after incorrect responses Fosters active inquiry and
                                               supportive interaction

Narrative: During the lecture, Ms. Wright asked several questions. A few students were actively engaged and did answer correctly. Most of the questions were not heard by the entire class because of the noise level. Ms. Wright did sustain incorrect responses and affirm correct responses.

Facilitating Instruction
Lesson plan meets requirements √   Provides for assessment of instruction

Narrative: Ms. Wright's lesson plans NCSCOS objectives were visible and in compliance.

Praise/Reflection/Strengths
Knowledge of content
Good questioning technique
Excellent board examples

Recommendations
Improve classroom management
Increase student monitoring
Establish and practice procedures for students' participation, students' movement and student discipline
Organize and plan more effectively

Before I received that Observation Checklist, I had my third observation and a major bust with the same group. When we met on the Tuesday the fifteenth of April, I was seething. I had hardly slept that night. In fact, I was hardly sleeping those days. When I finally dozed in the wee hours of the mornings, I was agitated and would be up before the alarm. I would curl up on the carpeted floor in the living room as I boiled water for tea and napped until the microwave sounded. I knew that the stress of the job was destroying me. My hair was falling out in clumps. I could pull out tufts with very little effort. It was showing on my skin too. My torso had a texture as if it had been burned. Sometimes I felt as though I could just go to sleep as I drove to work. It was during this time I realized how bad my eyes had gotten. I would see two men coming up the road and when I got nearer, I'd see only one. Or the speed limit would change as I neared it. Regardless of all these signs of my body's deterioration, I kept it together. My mind remained sharp and I assured myself that there were only two months to go.

It was already common knowledge that I would be leaving at the end of the school year. I had even been on an interview in Washington D.C., with some recruiters from England. In retrospect, perhaps I should have kept this information under wraps. But that's not how I operate. I remember how I waited for the school to sort out their affairs in order to know what teachers they needed so that they could contact me. Since I didn't like to be in that position, I wanted them to know my decision in good time.

Once again, I digress. Let me get back to the account. When they began to arrive for class on the Tuesday, I was waiting for them. One of the first to arrive started with her attitude. I told her to sit down and shut up with such force that my throat felt strained. I stifled a smile as she plopped into the seat and blinked in disbelief. She started to stutter and I told her to zip it, as I was not in the mood!

This was the problem. They have come to believe that this is the way that they should be treated. It was as though you were not doing your job unless you were shouting at them and being as abusive and miserable as they were. I like to talk to children and listen to them. If they have to be punished, then I'll punish them. I don't think we have to be crude and brash to be civil and kind or show we care or are in control. Moreover, these were sixteen- and seventeen-year-old students. Some were already parents!

When the whole class had arrived, I told them that I was well aware of what they had done the day before. They laughed and tried to play innocent. Then they started to confess.

"Miss Wright, you're too different. You never get mad."

"You teach different and we not used to that."

"We never know you understand our curse words; because we tell some other foreign teacher and they didn't understand them."

"You too nice, you gotta cuss dese kids."

"You give us too much work"

"I never talk to no Jehovah's Witness before."

What an insight I got into their little minds! I reminded them that education should teach them tolerance. If they understood that different is not bad, then they would not have wasted all that time by being mean and disagreeable. Surely they could still learn from me. Why would you want to be mean to someone who you think can't understand your language? What does it say about you as a person? We have to learn to be kind and meek which does not mean that we are weak. It takes great strength to demonstrate self control. We can't operate with such narrow minds. That was why we were considering cultures in the works of literature that we studied in class.

On that amenable note, we started class. Since we had not really done anything the previous day, we were going to complete some of the activities we should have done. Since we had muffled through the discussion on parables the day before, we started with the debate two of the characters in the story were having. The story is entitled; *How Much Land Does a Man Need?* It is set in Russia. I was hoping to integrate history, geography, religious knowledge and culture into this lesson. I wanted them to write their views to express which they thought was more advantageous;

life in the city or life in the country. They should give three reasons or examples for their response. This was not an essay that I was collecting. I wanted them to jot down their views and share them orally. After all, they needed to develop their speaking skills as well as their writing skills. However, I was awarding grades for their participation.

We were going through the sharing process and sometimes I would ask the speaker a question for clarity and one may lead to another depending on the response. These questions were designed to help them make their point more solid. Soon they started to quarrel that I was asking too many questions. I decided I would ask one question and a member of the class could ask another for clarity. They started to argue that the question was too long. I put down my foot and told them that we could not carry on like that, either they were prepared to learn and would allow me to do my job or they sit quietly and stop interfering. They started again and all the old complaints were being aired once more.

It was in the heat of this that Mrs. Burns came in the room. I was really not in the mood for another of these arguments. At one point they mentioned something from the first incident when Mrs. Burns was there and I said it was a good thing she was now present and could confirm what was said the first time.

"Don't talk about Mrs. Burns because you see her. That won't save you."

"Hey guys, remember that she is human—that's what she said. She be human—remember."

"Miss Wright, you think it is fair for the teacher to disrespect the students?"

"How have I disrespected you?"

"No, you can't answer a question with a question!"

"Mrs. Burns, will you please ask them?"

"So, in what way has Miss Wright disrespected you?"

"She treats us like animals." They may have heard my intake of air. "When she wants us to be quiet, she puts her finger on her mouth to say, shhh! Like we are little puppies—"

"Or she 'clap-clap-clap' like we are little animals." He had pasted 'dick' on my back.

I smiled and asked, "At what point do I usually do this?"

"Well, it's true that you will be holding up your hand for us to keep quiet and if we're not quiet, you treat us like animals."

Mrs. Burns turned her head away to hide her smile, and then explained, "So if you know that it is her signal for you to be quiet, you should follow it. Different teachers have different signs. Some may use a drum; others use music or some other procedure they would have agreed on. That is not being disrespectful. All this is wasting valuable time. What have you learnt in this time? Nothing, you could be doing better by doing the lesson planned."

We exchanged concerned glances. What utter foolishness is this? By their own admission, what I did was a last resort because they would have ignored what is procedure. The same procedure observers claim they never see.

I agreed with Mrs. Burns to an extent. I also believe that the students needed to talk in a non-combatant atmosphere. If they could believe that my treatment of them was disrespectful and less than humane, they needed more help than I thought. Mrs. Burns spoke to them some more and then she left. She said she didn't know what else to do with them. Imagine me dealing with them every day!

During the lunch break, one boy approached me and asked whether I noticed that he was not cursing me like the rest, nor did he behave like them. I told him that it didn't make him better, since he had done nothing to stop them, neither did he speak up on my behalf when Mrs. Burns was present. He admitted that he was just as culpable and we parted and went on our way. I hoped that he felt ashamed.

The following day, the Wednesday, those students came in class, sat quietly and went through the objectives and agenda. This was the same group of second block students who stood out because of their abusive speech, lewd conduct or threats toward me. This is the same group that Mr. Early had observed me with on Monday, when he found them "disorderly, very defiant and noncompliant."

Because I was operating the CD player and using the text and projector, I sat on the stool that the student had welded, so I had a wide view of the room. Everybody was quiet! Not one to look a gift horse in the mouth, I seized the day. I really went in the lesson especially with everybody being so attentive. They had gotten the vocabulary from the week before. These were synonyms for greed. They had also used them in a paragraph to show that they understood the nuances. I had them reflecting on the story in the context of the history of slavery in the United States.

Again, Mrs. Burns entered the room quietly, but we carried on as though she wasn't there. I felt the old feelings coming back. I was teaching! I was teaching! I played the CD. We read parts. I questioned to my heart's content. I explained. They responded and questioned in turn. Oh, the pleasant sound of paper rustling as they turned. When I gave them the task I moved around to check their progress. Mrs. Burns and I crossed paths at the back and we smiled. Why can't it be like this a third of the time?

"Excellent lesson!" she declared and the class erupted in applause. She went through the door and the students began to close the books. Just like that. Yet they were so pleased with themselves.

"Miss Wright, I learned a lot today."

"You could have been learning like this every day, if you would only be students and let me do my job instead of resisting," I replied.

After the declaration of it being an excellent lesson, I'm trying to decide if this evaluation reads more like the description of a mediocre lesson or a mediocre review of an excellent lesson.

Teacher Observation Checklist
April 16, 2008

Objectives: 1.02 Respond reflectively by relating personal knowledge to textual information. 2.02 Create responses that examine cause/effect relationship among events.

Instructional Time
When I entered the room, students were seated in desks and the teacher was seated on a stool in front of the class. Students used textbooks, paper, pen, and listened to an audio tape of a story. The time was 10:50.

Student Behavior
There were no inappropriate behaviors observed. Some students were eager to answer the questions and would begin to answer all at once. Ms. Wright would remind them of the fact that they need to raise their hand.

Instructional Presentation
Students listened to an audio tape on "How Much Land Does a Man Need?" Students followed along in their textbooks. Students were on-task and interested in the story as noted by the turning of pages and the responses given. Ms. Wright referenced prior discussions in helping students understand the content. On one occasion, she asked "What are the seven deadly sins?" A student named five of them. T. What was the word used here? S. Envious T. What other word did you hear? A student struggled to get the correct word, and the teacher finally helped her. The word was "avaricious." There was good interaction between the teacher and the students. Note: Was there some prior discussion of the vocabulary that would be found in the story? Students seemed to enjoy the lesson. At 11:15, students were instructed to make a sequence map to tell what happened from start to finish from the story. The class ended at 11:20.

Instructional Monitoring
Ms. Wright did not circulate about the room, but was seated so she could have a good view of the class.

Instructional Feedback
As students answered, Ms. Wright asked clarifying questions. She probed students for more elaboration. She responded on several occasions, "That is correct."

Facilitating Instruction
Lesson plans were not checked on this visit.

Praise/Reflection/Recommendations
Ms. Wright engaged the students by asking relevant questions. At one point, she asked "What would you do?"

Multiple instructional strategies were used.

One of the things that teachers must contend with today in this fast-paced world is the short attention span of students. In addition to this, is the problem of everything being so 'previous'. We see it in the news where before the president makes a speech, there are leaks or speculation about what he will say. People are dominated by this spirit of instant gratification and these days they are aiming for a pre-instant gratification, if it is possible. The world is so information-driven that some people seem to get a high from it; they are always impatient for a fix. It does not mean that they are smarter, or that the standard has risen, but that they want more and more of everything more quickly at the expense of quality.

How does the classroom teacher deal with this? We have to give in a little. Our planning must cater to satisfying some of these cravings and still be educationally nutritious. I had to widen my own experience in order to find what appealed to the students and use these things to get to them. You may have noticed how I tried to use technology—especially the DVDs—which was both entertaining and educational. I found out that it was a good way to get them interested in what they found to be old and sometimes pedestrian narratives. I always tried to find something for them to relate to in the stories. I would help them to see the same themes in movies that are current.

After we had read the story, *How Much Land Does a Man Need?* I bought the *Over the Hedge* DVD and prepared a checklist for the students to complete as they viewed it. When I submitted my permission slip, the receptionist told me that Mr. Early wanted to see me. They rarely wanted to see you for something good, so I stiffened my back for what was about to come.

"Oh yes, Miss Wright, I only wanted to tell you to be careful how you are showing these cartoons. It will cause the students to act up." He seemed to be saying it under a strain.

"I'm sorry, Mr. Early, but I must disagree with you. This is the only time I can sit in the class and have absolutely no problems with them. It is an animated movie which deals with some serious themes. But they are prepared for it. They are not watching merely for entertainment, but to see how current the themes from the stories are today." I didn't bother to tell him how the story line examines different types of greed among mankind and animals and how these adversely impact both species and the environment. The exercise was also helpful in achieving the objectives of the Pacing Guide. This is the check list that they were required to complete during and after the viewing. Note that the connection has been made to the story and the questions are set at different levels.

Movie Checklist
April 24 and 25, 2008

Objectives: NCSCS – 5.02 Demonstrate increasing comprehension and ability to respond personally to texts by:

i. Exploring a wide range of works which relate to an issue or theme of world literature.
ii. Documenting the chosen work.

5.03 Demonstrate the ability to read, listen to and view a variety of increasingly complex print and non-print literary texts maintain literary focus by:

i. Summarizing key events and/or points from text.
ii. Making connections between works, self, and related topics.

You have already read the short story, "How Much Land Does a Man Need?" View the movie, "Over the Hedge" and write your responses to the following prompts.

1. **Use the dictionary to provide the definition for the following words.**

   a. Pandemic---

   b. Amphibian--

   c. Extinction--

   d. Naïve---

   e. Impenetrable---

   f. Luminous---

g. Humane--

h. Vicious--

2. Explain what cause RJ to seek the help of the other animals ----------------

3. What is the name of the 'weird' thing? ----------------

4. What were some of the obstacles that Vern encountered when he ventured to the other side? --

5. What causes the food shortage among the animals in the forest? --

6. Explain any of the following phrases, based on what you have seen in the movie: a) *The grass is always greener on the other side.* b) *Enough is never enough* c) *Family*

7. How are RJ and Pakhom similar?

I hope that they will never forget the essential lessons in the combined exercises. This is what they would have missed if I had not stepped out of the box for a moment. I could have left the school at that point thinking that there were some redeeming aspects to my experience there. But you know what they say: When one door closes another one opens up somewhere. Who knows what or who will come out?

Mr. Ocheato had been threatening to come and see me for some time. He had been telling me for over a month. Somehow he was not able to come to my class until the day after the James-and-Bryan fight. By that time, we were reviewing for exam or end of course tests. In fact, some students had already started testing in their year groups.

A student was handing out graded papers when Mr. Ocheato entered the classroom. The chalkboard had the agenda and objectives as usual and we would review the work returned before going into the lesson for the day.

Here is what I can't understand to this day. This was my fourth official evaluation/observation and, although I had three groups of students, all three observations that would be admitted were with the same group. Remember that the first evaluation was not admitted. Now, here we go again.

Miss 'Banana Boat' was in one of her moods. She had completed the task while she was in ISS. I don't know who had sent her there, but she was either on OSS or ISS each week. Since I had received her paper at a different time from the others, it was in another folder. I didn't want to go to the desk to search for it because Mr. Ocheato was sitting there and we didn't need it since we were merely going over the work. I gave her a new one and asked her to use that until I could return hers.

"I didn't get my paper. I want my paper. You betta not lose my paper 'cause I need to pass this class. I did my work and you lose my paper…" she was just going on and on.

"Your paper was graded. It is with another set of papers. I will return it to you later. Now let's not waste time. You'll get it next class."

It was as if I had not spoken. She continued in the same exaggerated tone of mock anger. I knew it was a show. I went over to her and in a for-your-ears-only tone; I told her I'd had enough. If she kept up that charade, she would not like it. This is a student for whom I had marked a lot of make-up work, so that she could be in a position to pass the class. I had had conferences with her and the Social Worker that were productive. I had sent her to sit in Coach Major's class for time outs instead of writing her up sometimes. I didn't know how else to reach her.

We went through the returned work, and then they completed a short exercise to prepare them for the lesson. My best student was not feeling well. She had arrived sneezing and she was resting her head on the desk. A boy who lives in a group home was being his usual problem self. I had to call to him several times. We were proceeding as best as we could. Those who were participating were overcompensating. They were eagerly supplying responses sometimes without really giving the questions much thought.

Several times I had to hold up my hand, sometimes even turning my back to let them see that I was not listening. They would stop and we would continue. Other times I had to remind them: "Let's do the civil thing." They would get the drift and put up their hands if they wish to comment. But they are not machines and so their desire to share may overwhelm them. When that occurred and they shouted out their views before being called on, I'd ignore that response and take the same answer from someone else who had indicated.

Because the focus was on conflicts—external and internal— we were not short of ideas. I made reference to some external conflicts that they were aware of and asked Mr. Ocheato to point out the areas on the map where they had taken place, since he was sitting underneath the map. I made notes on the board of the ideas they were providing as we went along. We weren't starting anything new because exam was the following week. This was merely revision.

When I was helping them to plan an essay using the Thinking Map on the chalk-board, we ran out of space and they suggested that I could erase the agenda as they didn't need it. Some said I could erase the objectives too because they didn't need those either. I reminded them that there was another class to come and that I would not be able to rewrite them in time. After we had finished the plan, their task was to write the essay. Usually, this is the point I really get to move around instead of just half-way down the aisles.

If the truth is to be told, I had come to detest going among the students if they weren't occupied. Even then I was very wary and careful. This was the same group that had tagged me "Dick," under the guise of trying to get my attention. After that they had been calling me from one end of the class to the next to look at their work so that everybody could read and laugh as they viewed it from different angles. I had never seen them worked so diligently and had become suspicious.

In the fourth block, the boys may throw coins or paper balls at each other the minute I start heading down the aisle and some of them were out of my line of vision. Some would even sneak out the back door. The room is so small anyway that if I walk down the aisle, some boys would put their foot out in the path or their hand along the desk to cause me to brush against them as I walk back. It was simply uncomfortable. At this point I was just happy to be able to go through the lesson planned, collect the completed work and see that nobody hurt anybody.

During the lesson, it was 'Miss Banana Boat' again who claimed she did not understand me when I was—her word—

"conversating." I had given up trying to convince her that it is not a usual English word. She said, "See, you can't even talk English. What is bank? —It's beng-k! You can't talk. I don't know how you can be teaching English and you can't even call words properly."

I had been through this before. I was reading and had said the word "bag" and she had had a good laugh and proceeded to correct me. She didn't spell it, she sounded it for me, "It's bay-egg." I had her sound the vowels in all these words: BAG, BEG, BIG, BOG, BUG and encouraged her to say it before the mirror and watch her mouth change shape. There were real foreigners there from the Philippines and South America. I wonder how they did with their pronunciations. We know it was not about that because these students were watching Jamaican movies that I would not dream of watching and they understood every word. On the day Mr. Ocheato was present she put on a show. She turned to the others for approval as she oscillated between participating and disrupting. Then they call *me* mad? Ha!

When Mr. Ocheato left, his mouth led the way. His head was in the air and the muscle in his jaw was twitching. He left without a word. That Saturday was one of the make-up days and he brought me his postmortem report.

Teacher Observation Checklist
May 09, 2008

A check (√) indicates at standard. A negative (-) indicates below standard.

If an item is not marked, it was not observed during the observation.

Instructional Time

Materials √   class started quickly √   Time on task for learning -

Narrative: Class was already in progress. Materials consisted of; the textbook, chalkboard, paper, and pencil. There was valuable time wasted.

Student Behavior

Rules posted √   Frequently monitors behavior -   Stops inappropriate behavior -

Narrative: Rules and procedures are posted, however, most students fail to follow or just ignored them at all. The noise level was intolerable. Students talked out of turn and shouted their questions or concerns toward the teacher. Seven students were indifferent and oblivious to the activities. Six students put their heads down. The students closest to the front were somewhat engaged in the process. The teacher failed to acknowledge nor addressed inappropriate behavior. The class was almost chaotic in atmosphere.

Instructional Presentation

Lesson objectives visible in classroom √	Objectives stated at beginning of lesson	√ Links to prior learning √
Makes content meaningful; relevant examples	High rate of success on tasks	Brisk pace
Effective, smooth transitions	Adapts instructions to diverse learners	Assignment clear
Uses technology to support instruction	Students engaged, responsible for learning	
Provides closure to lesson	Develops critical thinking & problem solving skills √	

Narrative: The first activity was a bell work in which the students were asked to respond to questions on p. 137 of the textbook. The finished work was collected. It was followed with a teacher led discussion on the cultural and historical context of a story. A worksheet was used for this activity. Ms Wright was interrupted by students several times as she tried to explain the lesson. Very few students responded correctly. They plainly shouted what they thought were the correct response or examples. The third task was a review on writing an informational essay on conflict. Ms Wright reviewed the definition of conflict and the two types of conflict, internal and external. The teacher asked the class for examples of internal and external conflict. She also wrote the proper steps in organizing information on conflict prior to writing an essay.

Objective: to understand cultural and historical context of a story, poem, or other work of literature

Instructional Monitoring
Maintains deadlines, standards -   Circulates to check students' performance -
Poses questions clearly and one at a time -   Uses responses to adjust teaching

Narrative: Deadlines and standards were rarely maintained. Some students had a hard time understanding the questions from the teacher. The teacher was corrected twice by the students. Ms Wright stayed primarily close to the front of the class.

Instructional Feedback
Prompt feedback on work products √   Affirms correct response quickly √
Sustaining feedback after incorrect   Fosters active inquiry and supportive
responses   interaction

Narrative: Feedback on work product was scantily given. The teacher gave sustaining feedback on examples given by students. Correct responses were affirmed by the teacher.

Facilitating Instruction
Lesson plan meets requirements √   Provides for assessment of instruction

Narrative: Lesson plan conformed with local requirements.

Praise/Reflection/Strengths:

1. You, as a teacher, must establish proper procedure in this class.
2. Do not let students dictate to you what they want to take place.
3. You had a good lesson, but you failed to deliver.

Now that I have read his review of the lesson again, I think he had learnt quite a bit and a lot seemed to have taken place in that "chaotic atmosphere." If he was seated at the back of the class and heard so much of what went on, how noisy were we? How were we able to move through the different steps of the lesson? But that day I read the review during my lunch period and I could not eat after reading it. I felt as though there was a ball in my throat. My head throbbed as all the blood seemed to rush there to deal with the emergency which resulted from the jolt to my system. I wondered if Mr. Ocheato had been in the same room that I was in. I was sure of one thing—I was not signing it!

I set out to find Mrs. Williamston. When I got to her room she was not there so I proceeded to the bathroom. I needed to wash my face as it was burning from all that blood that had rushed there.

"Hi, Ms. Wright, wha' gwaan mon?" Mrs. Williamston had been learning some Jamaican expressions and was enthusiastically trying out this greeting. She immediately picked up that something was wrong. "What is it, dear?" she asked, concern registered on her face.

"Mrs. Williamston, please read this." She took it and began reading. I'll spare you her wrath, but suffice it to say, she agreed that the evaluation was mean spirited.

"I am not signing it because it is unfair and--" I choked up. Mrs. Williamston came forward and embraced me.

"Ooh sweetheart," her voice broke too.

As she held me at arm's length, I said, "I'm going to respond to this. I'm not signing it!"

"You go straight ahead, honey, umhum, it certainly deserves a rebuttal. I have been with those kids and they should not be in the regular school system. They deserve to be in a school by themselves. And what hurts is that he knows this!"

"Just imagine, I have missed only one day and one block of school since I've been here. I am never late. I always have my plans. I'm always making an effort in spite of the students and just look at what he saw!"

"You have not taken a day? Ms. Wright, that is amazing. How have you done it?"

She had to go on duty so we said our goodbyes. I think I was officially depressed. It is not a familiar emotion for me. That evening I felt strange in my body and I thought that it must be depression. I could not sleep and I could not cry and I desperately wanted to do both. I decided to set to work on the response. I read his checklist and indicated the areas of concern then wrote my response.

I showed it to Mrs. Williamston who inserted some commas and made two suggestions, but thought in general, that it was a good response. He called me to find out whether I had read his feedback and I told him that I would submit it later that day. I copied it to Mrs. Burns, Mr. Early, the two principals and Mrs. Williamston as Department Chair. Mrs. Burns was in the cafeteria so I told her that I would leave it in her office. I gave Mr. Early his in his hand and left Mr. Ocheato's on his desk. Strangely, everywhere I looked I saw him. He was in the cafe, coming down the corridor when I was at the office and at the corner of the building when I went to Mrs. Williamston. This was my response:

To:	Mr. Rob. Ocheato
From:	Ms. Marjorie Wright
Date:	May 31, 2008

Subject: <u>Response to Teacher Observation</u>

Please be advised that I refuse to sign the Teacher Observation instrument because I have found it to be insensitive and inaccurate.

Before I attempt to point out the many areas of contradictions and "nit picking," I would like to make these admissions: Firstly, that was not one of my best lessons. Secondly, the students are often abusive, defiant and disrespectful to me. Thirdly, since students often resist my methods of teaching, I may make concessions in order to maintain some peace in the classroom.

The fact that a number of them have missed school for disciplinary issues is clear indication that they misbehave with other teachers as well. I will not pretend to have control of them, and since your presence did nothing to deter them, that in itself is suggestive.

In addressing the areas of concern in your evaluation, I will try to respond to each area in your feedback. Please note that the date of your visit was the 29th of May and not the 9th as is stated on the instrument.

Time on task for learning is said to be below standard and you remarked that *"valuable instructional time was wasted."* The only time that was not spent on instruction was the time spent in addressing the students who were being disruptive. S—C—kept interrupting and was refusing to be reasonable. She had submitted her paper late, and it was graded, but in another set. She was upset because it was not returned. How else could this have been handled?

You accused me of not monitoring or stopping inappropriate behavior or ignoring students with their heads on the desk. H—B—was sitting sideways and was playing with Q—L--. He has been spoken to, removed from the seat and referred. He has just returned from ISS. I have had individual conference with Q—as well as with his parent. During the lesson I called to them several times. I even used the situation as an example of "conflict", the topic under discussion. Often when they are sent to the office, they return to class and a lack of action helps to undermine my authority.

J—G—has a cut in his palm and has refused to write or participate in class. C—H---often sits with his head propped on his bag on the desk; however, he does his work. T—and M—sometimes rest their heads on their desks, W—will even write in that position, and T—was not well. You may recall that I tried to get them involved by asking them direct questions. I know my students and choose my battles.

When we looked at the cultural and historical context, we compared methods of communication as well as the method of electing leaders. We compared how the village appointed a chief and how the USA elects a president.   In looking on external conflicts, we spoke of the forces of nature—earthquakes, cyclones, hurricanes and tornadoes we named China, Myanmar and USA. Are these relevant examples? I should think so!

You will recall that it was at this point that students pointed out that "tornadoes" was misspelled. They also told me of a word I was in the process of writing, in which I had written the initial letter twice. Their pointing out the error tells me that they were alert. I always thought, "to err is human; to forgive divine." I wish you had provided examples of some of the questions *"some students had a hard time understanding."* It is for this reason we have a discussion so that misunderstandings may be cleared up.

Earlier I said the evaluation was insensitive. I am forced to note your negative tone—the loaded words and absolute modifiers: *"noise level was intolerable," "teacher failed," "the class was almost chaotic", "feedback scantily given", "very few students responded correctly", "valuable instructional time wasted,"* etc. At the same time, you can point out evidence to the contrary. You noted that the bell work had been completed and collected. The teacher-led discussion generated responses which were acknowledged by *"sustaining feedback and affirmation by the teacher etc."* Under the circumstances, these were some good examples of progression and transition of instructional presentation.

In closing, I would like to reiterate that I disagree with many of your conclusions. I am disappointed that you could not have been more objective. When I consider the inadequacies of the system and the intolerance on the part of the students, I am pleased with my efforts. I turn up for work every day and I give it my best effort. A little support would be in order.

Marjorie Wright (Teacher)

CC: Mrs. Burns
Mr. Early

To this day I have never heard a word from any of those I had written to, although I heard that Mr. Ocheato had met with Mrs. Williamston. But that was that!

When I was called to the office for my cumulative evaluation, I was not sure what to expect. Mrs. Burns handed it to me and I read it.

"But Mrs. Burns, this is not entirely true!"

"You don't have to sign it, you know."

"No-no-no-no, I know where you're coming from and this is a different matter. You're alluding to the fact that I refused to sign the one Mr. Ocheato did. I'm not refusing to sign this. I'm merely asking that you write it to reflect the truth."

"What do you mean?"

"Anybody reading this will conclude that I was an incompetent teacher."

"Oh no, Miss Wright, you're an excellent teacher. You have a good grasp of the content; your instructional technique is excellent."

"But it's not reflected here!" My frustration was showing. "You, more than anybody, know what I was up against. You were there many days…"

"Well, you write it—there's a section for teacher's comment."

"I'll write it, but I also think you should document those observations you made earlier about my teaching. Here," I offered my journal the only paper I had with me "please write it."

"I'll write it tomorrow, OK? I'll write it tomorrow."

"You know something?" I asked, "I tell you this: If Leonardo da Vinci had inferior materials to work with, I doubt we would have seen his masterpieces today. Sometimes our art is as good as the quality of the material we have to work with." They say a poor workman blames his tools, but an excellent and fair one will acknowledge the deficiencies of his tools.

"That's true?" she responded, always avoiding my face.

"One more thing, the speaker at the Kingdom Hall the other night, related the account of the processionary caterpillar. He explained that they will follow the leader in a procession not deviating from the route. He related how a scientist in an experiment set them on a path and then put some food in the center near them, but they continued in the procession around the circle until they starved to death. The food was there all the time and they were hungry and very active, but all the activity was to no avail. The lesson—do not confuse activity with accomplishment!"

"That's interesting."

I finished writing my comment and shared it with her before signing it.

She asked, "Miss Wright, did you get a placement in England?"

"They have been sending me some schools, but I have not accepted any. They sound a lot like what I wish to leave here."

"So what will you do?"

"I could go home. I have no major debts and I should be able to go back to my old school, but I may just take a break. Either way, it doesn't matter."

So in the end, the Teacher Performance Appraisal read like this summary:

Based on the evidence from observation, artifacts, and discussion, the evaluator is to rate the teacher's performance with respect to the 8 major functions of teaching. The evaluator must add pertinent comments at the end of each major function for which a rating of *Above Standard, Below Standard or Unsatisfactory* **is given.**

Instructional Presentation, Instructional Feedback, Facilitating Instruction, Communication within the Educational Environment and Performing Non-Instructional Duties these six areas are all said to be At Standard.

Management of Instructional Time: **– Below Standard**

"Miss Wright struggled in her ability to keep students on task."

(I agree with this comment, but it begs the question: Why? How else could this be phrased to reflect the challenge that I was up against?)

Management of Student Behavior: **– Below Standard**

"Consistently apply rules and be less tolerable of inappropriate behavior."

(If I have to tell the students the same thing several times every day, then something is wrong with one of us. Shouldn't they learn this at some point? Is she suggesting that I was so tolerant of their behavior that I resigned? Imagine that! I established set rules and procedures, but was unable to sustain them because the line of support was broken. Students thought, for example that I treated them like animals when I applied the procedure for them to be quiet. When management undermined my authority and students showed no respect for me or management, what recourse did I have? Who could I turn to? It was not a case that these students did not know how to behave—they consciously chose to misbehave and it was often an orchestrated effort.)

Evaluator's Summary Comments: -

"Ms. Wright struggled in her management of student behavior. However, her ability to plan, work with staff, and in some cases, her delivery of instruction were plausible."

("However," was not necessary because a contrasting point was not made. Plausible means: believable and appearing likely to be true, usually in absence of proof: having a persuasive manner in speech or writing often combined with an intention to deceive.) I don't know about you, but in my book that says—you can't teach! It is a mere façade. Having seen their observation checklists, I'm not asking you to even look at my own accounts, focus on what they said in their narratives. Especially the last one which was the worst of the lot, can you say my Instructional Presentation was merely—plausible? The observers often get the sense of what was being taught and were able to name what marred the presentation, but they never said those were merely—plausible.)

I wrote: —**The students resented the fact that I was not an American teacher and so they rebel to show their resentment. In addition, the Course was based on writing and many of them did not like the process so they failed to remain on task.**

(Therein lies the struggle. How do you make people do what they don't want to do? This is "the land of the free" and these students may not know much, but they know that if they don't want to do something, you can't make them and they bravely defend that right.)

There was so much more that could have been said, but I realized it was a useless battle, so I gave up.

I could just imagine the report that my prospective employer would be getting. There was a certain degree of complicity among those in authority. Perhaps I was meant to be a kind of offering. I could be sacrificed to atone for their errors. Whatever the cause, I was out of there and I left them to their own schemes, designs and, hopefully, to their consciences.

Unfortunately, Mrs. Burns was not able to redeem herself. Her husband fell ill the next day and later died. I was saddened by the news and felt moved to visit with her before leaving NC. My housemate and I went in search of her home. Neither of us knew where she lived. Because Marilyn was in the habit of leaving for work later than I did, she would see Mrs. Burns' car turning at a point off the highway. We used this information and calculated the general direction in which she was living. We only got lost once. An old man by the church told us how to find the house. We were to look for the house with a wreath. I was really happy to find her at home. I had taken one of our publications for her: *When Someone You Love Dies*. We embraced and I expressed the desire to meet her under more pleasant conditions in the future. I would really like to hear her honest, objective perspective of everything.

I could not end this without telling you this interesting experience I had with perspectives when I was living on the University campus. Sometimes when I feel good about myself, I will give myself a treat. It doesn't have to be anything extravagant. This evening in particular, it was simply taking a luxuriating shower, after which I gently applied some lotion and other fragranced salve before going to bed.

The morning I got up and went to the communal bathroom, I was still feeling good. My hair was tousled. The form fitting black satin night dress I wore, had thin straps which were attached to the heart shaped line above my breasts. As I walked, I felt the lacy frills, which ran along the diagonal hem from mid thigh of one leg to the top of my calf on the other, rustling gently as I moved. The waist was slightly draped with a fuchsia sash.

On my way back from the bathroom, I saw Kerry, a household member. She was stumbling toward the bathroom and rubbing sleep from her eyes. Upon seeing me she asked in her hoarse morning voice, "A wha' wrong wid you misses?" She kept right on walking.

"A who?" Andrea's voice came from the dark bedroom, like an owl's.

"No Chutney—out ya wid him head fava fi mad woman an' in a big ol' black frock wid a big red tring tie roun' di waist!"

Every chance I get I share this account. I still marvel at the two contrasting images we both had of the same picture. We saw the same thing from a different point of view and look at the result! Or did we?

CHAPTER THIRTEEN

The Resignation

On the day of graduation, I had a special moment. Mrs. Williamston had invited me to a classroom where she had asked a few friends, including the other Jamaican teachers, to meet. I didn't know that they had planned this for me. While I was waiting outside a teacher from the Academy, who would sit in on our meetings from time to time, came over to me.

"Are you one of the Jamaican teachers?" she asked. I know I looked different because I was wearing a wig. I had started wearing them after my hair began to fall out.

"Yes, I am." I answered.

"I heard that one of you is leaving. I hope it's not that nice, young lady in English. Which one are you?" this should be interesting, I thought.

"I'm in English." She looked at me more closely.

"Don't tell me it's you! Why, you look different. Oh, it's your hair. My, you are beautiful. I'm so sorry dear for your bad experience here."

"Never mind, I think this too will pass."

We went inside and Mrs. Williamston made the presentation to me. It was a plaque for being an Outstanding English Teacher at the school. The plaque was tangible evidence that some people saw my worth, but I was especially heartened by the things she said, "I am delighted to stand here and speak in honor of Marjorie because, honey, you are an outstanding person in every respect. As your co-worker, I take great pleasure in sharing a glimpse into your percipient and exemplary character.

As my colleague, you demonstrate the highest level of teamwork, working diligently and persistently, making sure that no obstacle prevents your students or your department from succeeding." The other teachers nodded and my throat constricted. She continued, looking at the little group gathered, she said, "Umhum, she has very high expectations for all of her students, and she sincerely tries to inspire all children to reach their potential. Her leadership and professional skills are apparent in all of her interactions not only with students in a classroom setting, but also with students outside of the classroom setting."

By this time she was beginning to take on the preacher quality and her audience was the little congregation. They were saying, "It's true. It's true," and they nodded more vigorously as she warmed to her subject.

"Look, even though she did not have a class of seniors the Fall Semester 2007 and I did, she saw my desperation and came to my rescue when it was time for the seniors to give their oral presentations before the Boards. She not only volunteered to serve as a judge, but she also called several other people to serve as well."

I was really feeling embarrassed by all the attention by this time, but she was not finished. "I will never forget your kindness, compassion, and dedication not only to your students, but also to your co-workers. My dear, you truly are a paragon among your colleagues. Your participation and devotion transcends the normal requirements."

By this time my nose was beginning to water. I was trying to smile to see if it would stop. She was going between addressing me and telling the others about me. "Although she is very popular among her colleagues, she does not yield to pressure, thus earning the respect of her students, parents, colleagues, and administration." I thought that was pushing it. I tried to suggest that, but she told me that, in spite of what had happened, I had made an impression on the students. "Her compassionate character fails to inhibit her from remaining steadfast and adamant in her beliefs and from achieving her goals, even when facing opposing views or adverse situations."

She got that right, I thought and I closed my eyes as I recalled some of those oppositions and adversities.

"Miss Wright, your departure will be a bittersweet one. I applaud you for having a desire to move forward in your career, but at the same, I shall miss your professional demeanor, mild manner, and gentle persuasion." The others broke out in applause when she finished. She handed me the plaque and enveloped me in a warm motherly embrace.

Some of the students were also forth coming with their own testimonials. I overheard 'Miss Banana Boat' telling a boy who was boasting that if he had been in my class he would have gotten all 'A's. She said, "Oh no, in Miss Wright's class, you have to work for your grades."

These samples were especially revealing.

This first one was written by a student who had had to repeat the class. He also lived in a Group Home and showed great promise as a writer. He loved to read. There were behavioral issues and I had to meet with his adoptive parents and his guardian on a number of occasions.

June 09, 2008.
Dear English II Students,

I have learned of avarice, love, war, life and adolescence from the stories I have read in this years English II Course. Of the many stories here are a few, "How Much Land Does A Man Need?" "I Love a girl but she lives over there", "Thoughts of Hanoi", "Civil Peace", and "A Walk To the Jetty". Of the things I have mentioned that I have learned are from these stories.

The student of Ms. Wright's English II Class, can get the best from the program listening to Ms. Wrights directions, being attentive, and doing your work. By listening to Ms. Wright you learn from the best and contain all the necessary skills you need to pass this course. By being attentive you focus on just the subject and don't stay off course and what your supposed to do. By doing your work you can pass.

There are a few things I wish I had done differently and doing more classwork is definetely one of them. There are also a few things I wish I had done better and giving my all is one of them. Of the few things that I wish I had done differently and better, there are many things I would not change. Such as Ms. Wright being my teacher. Ms. Wright has taught me discipline which something I really needed.

I am glad I took this course because writing is one of my many strengths. By taking this course it has strengthened me. I would rather be moving forward instead of backwards and this is something I have definitely done in this course.

English helps in all areas of work and study because writing is in everyday life and deals with everything. I hope the next set of students learn as much as I did in this course.

W. B.

June 09, 2008.
To the English II students of 2008-2009:

Have you wondered what you will learn in this class? When I first got here I thought it would be just reading stories, answering questions, and listening to Ms. Wright lecture but it wasn't. Yes, we did do that, but that wasn't all, we read poetry, stories, we watch movies, we had a speaker come in and talk about the Vietnam war. If you pay attention to the theme and lessons in the stories, poems, and movies the class will become much easier.

For instense we read "How Much land does a man need", the theme was greed and at first I didn't realize it, then we watched "Over the Hedge", which brought greed to perspective and then I understood it. So maybe I didn't pay attention to the story shame on me but at least I got what was taught and it wasn't easy so keep your eyes on the teacher and not the childish people in class.

In all if I could take this class over I would have done more work, and payed closer attention because I think the real lesson in this class was missed even though I passed. So don't take this class for granted, it may help you in the future.

Anon.

Enlish Class
We have had a lot of fun In ms. Wright's class.
Even though 50 percent of us will pass
Now I wish I had paid attention
I did not learn very much but, I forgot to mention
That we all had learning chances
But, we talked and laughed and did silly dances
But, this class will help me again someday
Because I learned that I should work and not play
I read stories about love & heard about lies
I have seen how greed can make a grown man cry
It has been a long and rough ride for me

And I hope that in the end I will succeed.
To Ms. Wright I sayin good-bye to you
And I hope I do not repeat English II.

S. R.

Those were some of the feedback I got from a written assignment the students completed. No doubt there are those who in there retrospective moments will suddenly realize what they ought to have done. These in particular must be the ones to stand up and be counted and stop yielding to peer—pressure, but rather, be a force for good.

President Obama, speaking at the Hispanic Chamber of Commerce in Washington, had much to say about schools and teachers. He said:

"It is time to start rewarding good teachers and stop making excuses for bad ones... The future belongs to the nation that best educates its citizens ... I refuse to accept that America's children cannot rise to this challenge. They can, they must and they will meet higher standards in our time."

His dream is laudable, but he has a big problem. How will these schools achieve this goal with such myopic and prejudiced administrators? These people are demotivating good teachers and are sitting as guardians of faulty policies and procedures. They treat hardworking teachers unfairly by robbing them of a sense of achievement.

At this stage it may seem like I'm going overboard, but when I describe my experiences in this area, you will be forced to agree that there are basis for my claims. You will see that my claim is not merely plausible, but evident without any intent to deceive.

You'll recall that one of the main objectives in employing me was to help to improve the test scores. The schools test scores had been under thirty percent for years from what I was told. For the first time in many years, the year 2008 saw a dramatic increase to almost seventy percent.

The first indication that they didn't want to share the winnings was at a staff meeting where it was announced that the school had done very well and special congratulations were in order for Mrs. Williamston, who they claimed had most of the slow learners, but still managed to do well. Really now!

There was another line of approach. Mrs. Burns asked me to take in my student list so that she could do a correlation of the statistics. Spelling and math are not my strong points, but my rough reading says I had over fifty-five percent passes from my five classes combined. I never heard a word from her about the sum of the research.

It didn't end there. The coordinator of the Writing Course from the County Office saw me in the café and she said, "Mrs. Wright," (She always called me *Mrs.* Wright.) "Mrs. Wright, congratulations on the good scores in the Writing Test. Even though, we're still not sure, because schools did very well across the board this year. I want to let you know that if you weren't leaving, we would have kept you on."

Talk about giving it in one hand and taking it back with the other! How could I take pride in my job, my accomplishment or employers? How could I maintain my enthusiasm and sense of security?

Without realizing it I was doing something that good managers and administrators should do. It was the combined effect of this experience Mrs. Williamston related to me and a talk I heard at the Kingdom Hall about showing gratitude or showing yourself thankful, which motivated me.

According to Mrs. Williamston, her husband was in the habit of cutting wood for the older women in his congregation. One year he had to be away and one of the old women said to her, "If Pastor was around, I would have fire wood."

Not missing a beat, Mrs. Williamston went home, gathered her two little daughters and they went to the back of their land and cut the wood, loaded it into their truck and carried it to the lady's house. She and the little girls made several trips as they unloaded the wood for the old woman. When they were finished, the woman looked at it and said, "Pastor always put it in the shed for me."

Not even "thanks!"

So I wanted to show myself thankful. I wrote notes to Mrs. Burns, Mrs. Sanderson, and Mrs. Williamston, thanking them for dropping by occasionally, providing support and sympathizing with their position with the challenges they had each day. I had three classes; they had the school. I didn't assume that it was their job.

Two of the recipients told me how grateful they were for the feedback and how much they needed to hear that they were making a difference, and that they had the support from other members. Earlier I told you that I learn from the greatest teachers in the universe. Don't you find it interesting that although Jesus was a perfect teacher his administrator still found it prudent to say, "This is my Son, the beloved, whom I have approved."? Matthew 3:17 and "This is my Son, the one that has been chosen. Listen to him."? Luke 9:35.

I can do wonderful things after a genuine commendation. I grew up with the pithy saying: Encouragement sweetens labor. Mr. Noteworthy, the agency's Regional Director, thought I was looking for a utopia. Far from it, I was looking for realistic and honest administrators and children who were just a little less unaware and a little more sensible. If that is utopia then I guess he was right. What I experienced makes me more determined that I will not call them kids. What do kids become? I am hoping to find people who behave with humanity. So rather than being tolerant of those conditions, in the teaching profession in that school, I decided to leave. Yes, I chose to resign than become resigned to mediocrity.

The exit interview was the last hurdle before I could really call it a day. My only regret was that it was not a face-to-face interview, where I could have elaborated on the questions, and that the space was so limited. The Human Resource Personnel asked me whether it was the administration that was the problem. I started to tell her that it went beyond the immediate administrators. They are successful at what they do because those at the county office either support them or undermine them. She ushered me out of the building very quickly. Regardless of how many different personnel are brought into the system, if the strongly entrenched "principles" are not changed, then any effort is pointless. Someone has to be willing to rock the boat or take the bull by the horns. Some of the areas that need to be worked over were addressed in my response to their questions based on my own observations.

Exit Interview
June 02, 2008.

What led you to interview with us?

My agents informed me of the position and your interest. I wanted a school in the rural area.

Why did you accept our offer of employment?

The Principal told me of the school's thrust to redesign for excellence. I wanted to be a part of the effort.

Was the position offered to you properly described?

Yes. I learned of the school's objective to improve the Writing score and to start a STEM school.

Did you receive adequate support to perform your job?

The support was not coordinated. This disunity resulted in an undermining of the teacher's authority.

Did you have a professional working relationship with your immediate supervisor?

Yes. I could go to her for advice and we shared strategies that we found to be effective in the learning process.

If your separation was voluntary, what could we have done if anything, to lengthen your employment?

Improve the behavior of the students that disrupts learning and impedes progress. Behavior such as this reflected in this statement, "I don't have to listen to you—you is just a Jamaican teacher."

What impressed you the most about our school system?

The Professional Development Workshops are usually helpful. I appreciate the facilities to keep the lines of communication open with parents.

What impress you the least about our school system?

*The lack of accountability on the part of students, Student placement— too many low achievers are placed in the same group. The curriculum should meet the needs and interest of all students. Students should **all** have an object like the State Writing Test to work toward—not just **some** students.*

What did you like best about your job?

The system of preparing reports—it saves time and provides sufficient feedback.

What did you like the least about your job?

I did not like the students' intolerance to change; their disregard for authority, and their apparent disregard for morality (cheating, refusal to work etc.)

Before this I had never seen a letter of resignation. I had never written one before, so I had to do some research. It was interesting to see how we are encouraged to be the diplomat right to the end.

May 23, 2008

Re: <u>Resignation</u>

I regret to inform you that I will not renew my contract with the Bertie County School System for the 2008-to-2009 school year. In light of this, I will resign my position as teacher of English, effective June 13, 2008.

From our discussions, you know how much I would love to stay. Unfortunately, I can see no alternative to the resolution of the conflicts between my personal and career goals, except to accept a position that is more in harmony with my objectives.

It would be remiss of me if I did not express my gratitude for the opportunity you granted me to practice my art in your institution. I am especially pleased with the rewarding association I was able to develop with both administration and my coworkers. Thanks for the support and please be mindful that I will miss this camaraderie.

While in your employ, I had the privilege of sharing my culture. I was able to show a positive perspective of my country and to impact the lives of children who may never go there or may be motivated to visit. I also have a sense of pride and satisfaction in my share in the school's record performance in the State Writing Test. It was a challenging year in which I learned a lot and I am grateful.

I will pray for your continued success and will make special petitions for those of you who are taking the lead. Please provide similar support for my successor because this task of teaching Writing is especially challenging. I hope you can also wish me well. Thank you once again for the opportunity. I will always value this experience.

Yours truly,
Marjorie Wright

Made in the USA
Middletown, DE
11 November 2022